Advance Praise for
Joel Simon's *We Want To Negotiate*

"A wise and thorough investigation of the painful conundrum posed by terrorist kidnappings. Simon makes a cogent argument about how to change our current, failed approach to negotiation."

—Lawrence Wright,
author of *The Looming Tower* and *The Terror Years*

"In *We Want to Negotiate*, Joel Simon combines the breadth of his knowledge alongside stunning narratives to try to understand how the gruesome and murky trade of kidnapping really works. Simon's international policy expertise and his compassion for his subjects—many of whom he knew and worked alongside—shine through to create a spellbinding, chilling, and important read."

—Janine di Giovanni,
Senior Fellow, the Jackson Institute of Global Affairs,
Yale University, and author of *The Morning They Came for Us:*
Dispatches from Syria

"A persuasive argument that deserves to be heard in Foggy Bottom, the Pentagon, and other corridors of power."
—*Kirkus Reviews*

"This is an excellently researched and reasoned book on a terrible and complicated problem: what to do when someone is taken hostage. I hope all those who have had to face this awful dilemma will read it, and especially those who make and carry out government policy."

—Terry Anderson,
author of *Den of Lions*, hostage in Lebanon for seven years

"Joel Simon has written an invaluable insider's account of the how and the why of the shadowy business of ransom negotiation at the highest level. For anyone who has ever wondered why some governments negotiate for the release of their captured citizens, while others—including our own—do not, Simon's book is essential reading. As head of the Committee to Protect Journalists, Simon has seen the hostage crisis up close and this book reflects his intelligence, courage, and clear-eyed approach to this murky but, sadly, thriving business."

—**Kati Marton,**
author of *Wallenberg, Hidden Power*, and *The Great Escape*

"Joel Simon's book about the dark world of kidnappers and their hostages is deeply reported, well written, and well calibrated in its judgments. For anyone who wants to understand the many difficult questions raised by the kidnapping trade, Simon's book will be the standard."

—**Peter Bergen,**
author of *United States of Jihad: Who are America's Homegrown Terrorists and How Do We Stop Them*

We Want To Negotiate
The Secret World of Kidnapping, Hostages, and Ransom

COLUMBIA GLOBAL REPORTS
NEW YORK

We Want To Negotiate
The Secret World Of Kidnapping, Hostages, And Ransom
Copyright © 2019 by Joel Simon

Published by Columbia Global Reports
91 Claremont Avenue, Suite 515
New York, NY 10027
globalreports.columbia.edu
facebook.com/columbiaglobalreports
@columbiaGR

Library of Congress Control Number: 2018949787
ISBN: 9780999745427
E-book ISBN: 9780999745434

Book design by Strick&Williams
Map design by Jeffrey L. Ward
Author photograph by Rebecca Greenfield

Printed in the United States of America

We Want To Negotiate

The Secret World of
Kidnapping, Hostages, and
Ransom

CONTENTS

Introduction

During the nearly two decades that I have worked at the Committee to Protect Journalists, my job has been to defend the rights of the journalists around the world. Kidnapping and illegal detentions are among the most common threats. I've worked on dozens of such cases, many involving international journalists.

In late 2002, *Wall Street Journal* reporter Daniel Pearl was kidnapped in Karachi, Pakistan by Al Qaeda. In 2003, *Los Angeles Times* photographer Scott Dalton, along with a British colleague Ruth Morris, was kidnapped in Colombia by FARC guerrillas. In 2006, Jill Carroll, a reporter working for the *Christian Science Monitor,* was kidnapped in Iraq. In 2008, Canadian journalist Amanda Lindhout and her Australian colleague Nigel Brennan were kidnapped in Somalia. That same year, *New York Times* reporter David Rohde and his two Afghan colleagues disappeared while reporting in Afghanistan.

In some of these cases, publicity was deemed to be helpful. So we cranked out press releases, did media interviews, and

developed strategies to put pressure on the kidnappers by
building public sympathy. In other cases, the families or the
media companies asked for discretion, and we honored such
requests, putting out limited information or none at all.
Sometimes, the journalists were freelancers who did not have
a media company to stand up for them. I recall a number of
instances in which I had to mediate complex family situations, involving divorced parents, exes, and concerned friends,
none of whom were clear about who was supposed to make
decisions.

Responding to a kidnapping puts a tremendous strain on
even the best-managed media company. It is all but impossible
for a family to bear. This fact hit me directly in the spring of
2014, when I got a call from David Rohde. Diane and John Foley,
the parents of journalist Jim Foley, were coming to New York.
They wanted to see me.

Jim Foley had disappeared in Syria in November 2012, and
for a time nothing was known about his whereabouts. CPJ had
learned that a number of other international journalists had gone
missing in Syria around the same time. We knew something bad
was up, but we were not sure what. We had been asked not to
publish any details about some of the missing journalists but
finally, in order to alert other journalists about the danger, we
put out a press release noting the high number.

We were certainly aware of Jim's case, as he was a personal
friend to many at our organization. I had met him briefly at a
photo exhibition in Manhattan. Since Jim's kidnapping in Syria,
we had been working closely with Phil Balboni, the publisher of
GlobalPost, where Foley worked. We offered our help and advice,
but since Balboni was working behind the scenes with a private

14   security consultant, there wasn't much we could do other than
       publicly express our concern.

       Now, after eighteen months with little progress, Diane and
       John had decided to try to raise a ransom to free Jim. They were
       looking to produce a video and asked for my help. Their idea was
       to show the video at fundraising events, or even screen it for
       individuals in a position to make a pledge. John and Diane asked
       if I could find a filmmaker who would take this on. The first sev-
       eral I approached turned me down flat because of the perceived
       legal risk. Finally, I found a young filmmaker through a contact
       at Columbia University who agreed to help shoot interviews.
       We converted the CPJ conference room into a mini-studio,
       and invited Jim's friends and colleagues to come by and pro-
       vide their testimony. We gave this footage to Diane, who even-
       tually found another filmmaker in California to create the final
       four-minute video.

       But the fundraising effort never really got off the ground.
       In August, Jim was dead. The video was shown at a memorial
       service held for Jim in October near his family home in Roch-
       ester, New Hampshire. I'm sure I was one of the few people in
       the room who know its intended purpose.

       John and Diane, and all of the Foley family, showed tremen-
       dous strength and fortitude following Jim's death. They spoke
       at the CPJ gala dinner in November 2014, during which we
       remembered Jim. But colleagues began telling me that in private
       Diane was quite critical of CPJ's role. So I asked about her con-
       cerns. She told me that CPJ did not do enough for Jim, and that
       she was disappointed. I conceded that we could have done more,
       but also explained why we were constrained. At the time CPJ
       had a policy of discouraging the payment of ransom—especially

by governments—because we believed that paying ransom   15
could lead to additional kidnappings, increasing the risk for all
journalists. I also had personal concerns about the legal risks to
me and to the organization if we were directly involved in any
fundraising effort, since the money raised would go to a terrorist group.

Prompted by Diane, we began a review process. We asked a
lawyer who had volunteered her time to assist CPJ in researching
the rationale for the U.S. no concessions policy, which affirms
that the U.S. does not "negotiate with terrorists." But this was
only the beginning of what has become for me a much more
sweeping and comprehensive undertaking. Different countries
take different approaches to the kidnapping of their nationals.
Some take a hard line, and others are willing to talk. I wanted
to understand not only which approach was more effective, but
also the moral and political consequences of providing funding
to a terrorist organization. And I wanted to look not only at
the issue of ransom, but also the structures for analyzing and
responding to intelligence and providing ongoing support for
hostage families.

It's important to put the issue of hostage-taking in the
proper context, especially because it's so highly emotional.
First, the vast majority of kidnappings around the world are
criminal in nature. Reliable numbers are hard to come by
because many criminal cases go unreported. But just to give
some context, more than 1,700 criminal kidnappings were officially recorded in Mexico in 2013, a record year in that country.
Authorities concede that the actual number is at least ten times
higher. One Mexican activist estimated the total 2013 kidnapping victims at 27,000.

That tally, if accurate, would be vastly more than the total number of terrorism-related kidnappings carried out in the last few decades, although again that precise number is not known. According to a December 2015 study from the Combating Terrorism Center at West Point there were 7,048 kidnappings perpetrated by what are called non-state actors between 1970 and 2013. Non-state actors include terrorists, but also militant and tribal groups and even pirates. The overwhelming majority of these cases were domestic. That means Syrians were kidnapped in Syria and Colombians were kidnapped in Colombia.

The West Point study did find a surge in terrorist kidnapping since 2001, fueled by increases in domestic cases in regions where Jihadi organizations were active, mostly the Middle East, Africa, and Asia. From 2001 to July 2015, there were 657 kidnapping incidents involving Westerners, an average of about 45 per year. In other words, the kidnapping of Westerners by terror groups is a small subset of the overall problem. But those cases are the focus of this book because they have the ability to influence global policies and provide significant financial support to transnational terror groups whose actions impact millions.

Because of my background, many of the cases featured in this book involve journalists. But my intention is to use those cases to illuminate the issues. My conclusions apply to all cases of kidnapping, journalists or not. I focus on kidnapping by non-state actors, terror groups, and transnational criminal groups. But I also briefly discuss hostage-taking by states—the detention of a foreign national on trumped up charges in order to gain a political concession. Such practices are common in North Korea and Iran.

As noted, the kidnapping of Westerners by terror groups is
a relatively rare event. But this is not simply a numbers game.
Kidnapping comes in cycles, and each cycle responds to its own
dynamic. Kidnappings can be used to achieve a variety of objec-
tives. They can generate revenue through ransom; they can be
used to extract political concessions; or they can be used to sow
terror and fear. Kidnapping thrives in lawless places in the midst
of conflict. When motive and opportunity come into alignment,
kidnapping surges. This is precisely because it is such an effective tactic. There are periods of calm, but it always returns, often
in a more brutal form.

My analysis is global, but I deeply researched several countries that highlight a range of approaches. France has a reputation for being the country most willing to pay ransom for
hostages, but my own investigation shows that its policy is
actually more nuanced. The key variable in determining the
government's response is the level of popular mobilization on
behalf of the hostage. Spain, meanwhile, experiences no such
conflict. The task assigned to the country's intelligence service
is to bring hostages home at all costs. Because of its willingness
to pay, the country has a tremendous record of success. The UK
and the U.S., meanwhile, are the leaders of the no concessions
camp. They do not pay, and in many cases, do not negotiate. As
a result, a high number of British and American hostages have
been killed. These countries ask their citizens to make this sacrifice because, they believe, to do otherwise would encourage
more kidnapping and funnel resources to terrorists that would
be used to finance future attacks.

Because of the sensitivity of the issues addressed in this
book, many key sources asked to speak to me on background. In

18   nearly every case I agreed, though I also pushed back to see if we
      could put portions of those conversations on the record. Where
      that was not possible, I sought to corroborate the information
      provided through other sources. At the end of the day, however,
      more information is attributable to anonymous sources than I
      would have liked. My goal is to deliver into the public domain
      whatever is possible to ensure an informed policy debate.

          One argument that I often heard against public disclo-
      sure of hostage negotiations and ransom payments is that such
      information benefits the criminals. For the most part. I dis-
      agree. It certainly applies to active hostage situations, which is
      why I have not covered any in this book. But once the case is
      resolved, the real concern for governments seems to be polit-
      ical. The kidnappers already know how much money was paid
      and how negotiations were handled. It's the public that's in the
      dark. People cannot make informed decisions about whether
      their government acted prudently and responsibly without this
      essential information.

          On November 26, 2013 a year after he went missing in Syria,
      Jim Foley's brother Michael, along with Phil Balboni of *Global-
      Post*, received an email from his captors. It read, in lowercase
      letters, "hello. we have james. we want to negotiate for him. he
      is safe: he is our friend. we do not want to hurt him. we want
      money fast." It is from this message that the title of this book
      is drawn. After more than a year of research, I still do not know
      if that offer was sincere. But it does raise important questions.
      Negotiating with a terrorist group, even when a life is on the
      line, is never a straightforward decision. There are moral, polit-
      ical, and policy implications of the highest magnitude, partic-
      ularly for governments. But whatever decision is made, it must

be based on an objective consideration of the facts. Through a
journalistic exploration that includes interviews with former
hostages, their families and employers, policymakers, intelligence officials, law enforcement, and academic experts, that's
what I hope to provide.

The Hostage Advocate

When French journalist Florence Aubenas was kidnapped in Baghdad on January 5, 2005, along with her Iraqi colleague Hussein Hanoun al-Saadi, she was one of France's leading war correspondents. Over the course of eighteen years at *Libération,* a left-leaning French daily founded by Jean-Paul Sartre in 1973, Aubenas had covered conflicts in Rwanda, Kosovo, Algeria, and Afghanistan. But the rallies, protests, and media campaigns carried out in France in support of Aubenas while she was in captivity would make her a household name in her country. After her release she would go on to use her new celebrity to become a fierce advocate on behalf of French hostages. This was vital, because Aubenas's abduction came at the beginning of a surge in kidnappings and hostage-takings by criminals and terror groups. The successful effort to bring Aubenas home helped define France's approach to hostage-taking, and shaped the global response.

After Aubenas and Hanoun were taken at gunpoint, they were driven to one private home and then another. They never

learned the name of the group that was holding them. We are   21
"mujahidin combating the Americans in Iraq," was the only
thing her kidnappers told her. They locked her in a tiny, dank
room in a building's basement and made her wear a grey sweat
suit emblazoned with the word *Titanic*. She was blindfolded and
forbidden to speak. Hanoun was kept in the same room. Because
the hostages were held in near complete silence neither was
aware of the other's proximity.

In France, Aubenas's kidnapping was a huge national story.
Portraits of Aubenas and Hanoun were hung in the Place de
la République, and from public squares in France and across
all of Europe. Supporters rallied in front of the Eiffel Tower.
Muslim students from all over France organized a meeting of
solidarity and support at the Grand Mosque in Paris. The press
freedom organization Reporters sans frontières (RSF) and
Aubenas's newspaper *Libération* organized a benefit concert at
the 2000-seat Olympia theater, featuring top talents like Alain
Souchon and Patrick Bruel. On the hundredth day of their captivity, every broadcaster, every French radio station, and nearly
every media outlet in France made a coordinated public appeal.
Brass bands across France participated in an event dubbed
"1000 Fanfares" for the hostages.

The French government was prepared to negotiate, but it
was not able to make contact with the shadowy group that had
kidnapped Aubenas and Hanoun. RSF General Secretary Robert
Menard traveled to Aleppo and Beirut of his own initiative and
without government support, to meet with the Grand Mufti
and representatives from Hezbollah. His efforts to open a communications channel came up empty.

22   On March 1, the kidnappers reached out in their own brutal way. They delivered a grainy video to news organizations in Baghdad. It showed Aubenas, gaunt and disheveled, begging for her life. "Please help me. My health is very bad. I'm very bad psychologically also," Aubenas said in English, as she sat against a dark background with her knees pressed up against her chest. "Please, it's urgent now. I ask especially Mr. Didier Julia, the French deputy, to help me. Please Mr. Julia. Help me! It's urgent, help me!"

The reference to Didier Julia was an indication that the kidnappers were also looking for a communication channel. Julia was a member of the French parliament and an Arabic speaker. He had relationships with officials in the former government of Saddam Hussein, many of whom had joined the anti-U.S. insurgency. But the French government negotiators didn't trust Julia and didn't want to use him as an intermediary. On March 3, Julia was summoned to the office of the French spy agency Direction générale de la sécurité extérieure (DGSE) and questioned. He was later told to butt out. Incensed, Julia claimed the DGSE "didn't want Florence to be freed because she knows too much." His request for a meeting with President Jacques Chirac was rebuffed.

With Julia pushed to the sidelines, French negotiators hit a dead end. Didier François, a colleague of Aubenas's, was concerned. Like Aubenas, François had covered conflicts from Kosovo to Chechnya. He was known as a "grand reporter," an informal honor bestowed on France's leading war correspondents. François had set up the Baghdad bureau of *Libération* following the 2003 U.S.-led invasion. When Aubenas arrived, she found the office looked like a student dorm, with "his karate films, his whole little universe."

With the life of a colleague on the line, François made a decision to step out of his journalistic role. He hoped he could use his journalistic connections to open up a line of communication between the hostage-takers and the French government.

The process took months, and involved travel to both Jordan and Syria. French officials insisted that François sign an agreement that he would not use any information obtained through his mediation efforts in his reporting. Once the line of communication was open, the French government negotiating team, lead by the DGSE, took over.

On June 12, Aubenas and Hanoun were freed. Aubenas was put on a plane to Paris. President Chirac traveled to Villacoublay Air Force base to greet her. Photos of their warm embraces were splashed across French media and around the world. Back in Baghdad, Hanoun's family slaughtered a goat for a celebratory meal. Later, Hanoun traveled to France with his wife and son for a well-documented reunion with Aubenas.

Two days after her release, Aubenas, along with *Libération* editor Serge July, presided over a packed press conference at the Press Club in Paris. Dressed elegantly in an embroidered blue blouse, her sunglasses pushed up onto her dark hair, Aubenas struck a dramatic contrast with her harrowing image in the March hostage video. She was ebullient, funny, and self-deprecating. Aubenas thanked the media, the public, and her family for their unwavering support, even as she described her grim experience. "What it's like to live in a cellar?" she said in response to one question. "It is a very long experience to live, but a very short one to explain. What would I do? I would count. Count the days, count the hours, the minutes, the steps, the words, everything."

24   She was also able to count on the support of the French government. In the shadowy global world of hostage-taking, no country has more of a reputation for paying ransom than France.

The Times of London reported that France had paid $10 million for the release of Aubenas and Hanoun. Robert Menard told the AFP, "There is no hostage release without something in return and, among the demands, there is obviously a demand for money." When I spoke to Menard, he told me he had no specific information. Officially, the French government denied paying ransom.

Twelve years later, I met Aubenas in a Paris café. The sun was pouring in through a plate-glass window, creating a nearly intolerable greenhouse effect. Despite the heat, Aubenas insisted on sitting in the sun. Unlike many kidnapping survivors, Aubenas has no desire to talk about her own experience. She has no doubt that a large ransom was paid, but does not know the details. She has never written about her kidnapping, and she has spoken about it only in passing.

Partly this is because she does not want to give any satisfaction to her kidnappers, who told her that one day she would write a book and be "more famous than Lady Di." Partly, it's a desire not to allow herself to be defined as a victim. "It's sometimes difficult to have everyone see you as an ex-hostage every day," Aubenas admitted. "I prefer to act for people still in dangerous situations rather than know what exactly happened to me. Now I'm safe, and that's okay."

As a leading journalist and the author of a best-selling book on the fate of French workers, Aubenas has remained in the public eye. She is committed to using the visibility she gained through her own ordeal to help other hostages. Part of her commitment is heading what are called "support committees." These are informal structures set up by the families of hostages. Aubenas is often the first choice to lead such efforts. "Families choose someone to be the head of the committee who is well known in this country," Aubenas explains. "It's better if it is someone without problems and not too controversial. Someone who knows the topic and better still if they are a kind of friend."

Of course Aubenas's willingness to lead the support committees reflects her commitment to the families of French hostages. But it also reflects something larger. Aubenas believes that a willingness to negotiate and even to pay ransom is an affirmation of French democracy. She is concerned that the resolve of the French government to bring hostages home has sometimes wavered and that it is her responsibility to remind the French leadership of its obligation.

Aubenas's abduction was part of a wave that swept through Iraq beginning around 2004. This wave marked the emergence of a new era of political kidnapping that has posed extraordinary challenges to governments around the world. Kidnapping for ransom and to extract concessions has been a political practice for thousands of years. It has helped fund large-scale criminal enterprises, from the Barbary Pirates to the Mexican drug cartels. In recent decades, it has been a key source of funding for militant and revolutionary groups, ranging from Basque separatists in Spain, to the Red Army Faction in Germany, to the Montoneros in Argentina. The inherent drama of kidnappings has often captivated the public imagination, like the Lindbergh baby and the Patty Hearst case.

Political kidnapping requires a level of organization and infrastructure: A group must be able to capture the hostages, hold them for an extended period, communicate demands, and manage the ransom payment. Hostage-taking was a favored tactic of radical leftist groups operating in Europe and Latin America in the 1960s, was adopted by pro-Palestinian militants in the next decade, and became a defining feature of the Lebanon conflict in the 1980s. Between 1970 and 2013, there were 1,021 political kidnappings in Colombia, according to the Global Terrorism Database at the University of Maryland, which is compiled from open source records. Colombian human rights groups, which track kidnappings carried out by leftist guerrillas, right wing paramilitaries, drug traffickers, and run-of-the-mill criminals, put the number astronomically higher, at 40,000 kidnappings during this period. The discrepancy between the two figures suggests why it is prudent to see the available data as a comparative baseline rather than a definitive tally. The Global Terrorism Database, which provided much of the data for the 2015 report on global kidnapping published by the Combating Terrorism Center at West Point, recorded 732 kidnappings in India from 1970 to 2013, largely carried out by Kashmiri militants. There were hundreds each in Pakistan, Afghanistan, the Philippines, and Iraq. Most of these were carried by Islamist groups, some inked to global networks such as Al Qaeda. Following the September 11, 2001 attacks and the invasion of Iraq in 2003, there was a surge in kidnappings carried out by non-state actors, which rose from an average of 164 incidents a year to a high of 630 incidents in 2013. However, nearly all of the increase can be attributed to increased kidnapping of local nationals, not Westerners.

Unquestionably the rise of interconnected Jihadi movements transformed the landscape. Jihadi networks discovered that they could use new communications technology to place unprecedented pressures on governments, by releasing or threatening to release terrorizing videos that could be broadcast and shared all over the world, engendering fear on a global scale.

In January 2002, Al Qaeda militants in Pakistan kidnapped and murdered *Wall Street Journal* reporter Daniel Pearl. Previously, Al Qaeda had cultivated the favor of international journalists, hosting press conferences and granting exclusive interviews, like the ones Osama Bin Laden once gave to CNN and ABC. Pearl's abduction marked a shift (though it was largely opportunistic, as it came about because a source that Pearl contacted in the course of his reporting was actually an Al Qaeda operative). Pearl's murder was a spontaneous and improvised decision taken by Al Qaeda's propaganda chief, Khalid Sheikh Mohammed, the mastermind of the 9/11 attacks. Pearl's videotaped beheading—which was actually a reenactment because the camera jammed on the first take—sent a message to Jihadi groups around the world that kidnapping Westerners was now a sanctioned tactic.

Kidnapping and hostage-taking next emerged amid the post-invasion chaos in Iraq. The 2004 videotaped beheading of U.S. contractor Nick Berg by Al Qaeda in Iraq leader Abu Musab al-Zarqawi along with the execution of the Irish-born aid worker Margaret Hassan set a brutal tone. But the kidnappings that swept through the country were carried out by a range of intersecting political and criminal groups with varying motivations. Some who had earlier executed their victims without demanding a ransom began looking for a payout.

28   An analysis carried out by Norwegian researcher Thomas Hegghammer looked at 63 kidnappings, involving 159 victims in Iraq during 2004. Hegghammer described a classic case of "contagion," in which terrorist groups copied and learned from one another. Kidnapping, Hegghammer noted, is an effective tactic because it demands relatively few resources compared to suicide attacks and car bombings. It's useful as a propaganda tool because specific demands can be made and widely publicized. Because hostage situations play out over time, these demands can be "recycled" and used again and again. Unlike bombings, abductions can be used as a basis for negotiation, which may bring political and material benefits. The newly developed ability to publicize demands online allowed kidnappers to bring them to a global audience without relying on traditional media.

The "contagion" would soon spread through Islamist networks around the world, fueling international kidnappings in Afghanistan, Syria, Somalia, Yemen, and North Africa. A 2017 study carried out by New America Foundation counted nearly 1,200 separate kidnappings carried out by terrorist and militant groups between 2001 and 2015. This is certainly a low estimate, as many such incidents were never publicly reported.

The question of how to respond to kidnapping by terrorist groups and whether to pay ransom raises a host of political, moral, and strategic complications. Different countries respond based on their own laws, political traditions, and interests.

Many continental European countries, including Spain, Italy, Germany, Austria, and Switzerland, place an emphasis on the "right to life," a concept enshrined in European human rights law. They recognize that ransom payments can be used for terrible purposes but these countries are guided by a different set of strategic considerations. France, for example, did not participate in the invasion of Iraq and for the most part the insurgent groups operating there were not directly targeting France or French interests. When Islamist militants in North Africa kidnapped a group of thirty-two tourists that included sixteen Germans in 2003, the German government facilitated a 5 million euro ransom payment disguised as aid money. Following the beheading of Italian freelance journalist Enzo Baldoni in August 2004, Italy put in place an intelligence network to facilitate ransom payments. It was used to liberate Italian aid workers Simona Pari and Simona Torretta, and journalist Giuliana Sgrena.

But there was another reason France and other European countries ponied up that had nothing to with moral principles or strategic interests: It was politics. When French citizens are kidnapped, the public often mobilizes to demand their release. It's a tradition that goes back to the Lebanese hostage crisis, one that the French authorities initially encouraged. During a decade-long period from 1982 to 1992, cells linked to Hezbollah, Islamic Jihad, and ultimately the revolutionary regime in Iran took more than a hundred hostages in Lebanon, most of them from the U.S. and Western Europe. Among them were U.S. journalist Terry Anderson and British envoy Terry Waite, whose cases generated considerable interest and attention in their respective countries. But the fate of four French hostages, seized in the spring of 1985, became a national obsession.

On May 22, 1985, kidnappers from Islamic Jihad intercepted the airport taxi carrying journalist Jean-Paul Kauffmann and sociologist Michel Seurat. The kidnappers trundled them into a car and took them to an underground parking garage. They

30   were held along with a pair of French diplomats who had been nabbed two months before. When Seurat died of cancer seven months later while still in captivity, his captors lied and claimed he had been executed. The ruse was intended to increase public pressure, and it may have worked. The three remaining hostages were released on May 2, 1988, in exchange for significant political concessions by France. These included the unfreezing of Iranian assets, the expulsion of the Iranian opposition from France, and the eventual pardoning of a prominent militant imprisoned for an assassination attempt against the former Iranian Prime Minister (who was living in exile outside Paris).

During their three years of captivity, Kauffmann and the other French hostages "were featured every night at the beginning and the end of the nightly news," recalled Hala Kodmani, the Middle East editor at *Libération*. Their release was presented as a major victory for French diplomacy and for President François Mitterrand. A high-level government official greeted the returning hostages. "The French public is very sensitive to the idea of a French citizen being abducted," said Kodmani. "Mitterrand made a big show at the airport. He set the precedent, and it continues today."

Since then, the kidnapping of a French citizen abroad has been seen as *une affaire d'état*, not merely an attack on the hostage's family or employer but an attack on French interests. At the heart of France's political culture is the belief that the state has the responsibility to protect the well-being and security of French citizens. The power to take decisive action on behalf of French citizens abroad—including authorizing ransom payments—is conferred on the office of the president. In part, this is a legacy of France's colonial past, but it is also a recognition

that France's soft power is expressed through its cultural and
economic relationships throughout the world.

The context for international kidnapping has changed dramatically since the Lebanese hostage crisis. The kidnappings carried out by radical Shia groups like Hezbollah and Islamic Jihad in the 1980s served a fundamentally political purpose. Under the guidance of Iran's Revolutionary Guard, the hostages were used to achieve strategic leverage in the ongoing conflict with Israel and also to win the release of jailed militants. Hezbollah and Islamic Jihad targeted prominent individuals and developed a clandestine infrastructure that allowed them to hold hostages for extended periods while they carried out negotiations. In this environment, public mobilization helped the French government put pressure on the hostage-takers—who sought some level of international legitimacy for their cause—while giving it the political cover it needed to engage in proxy negotiations with Iran.

But the calculus was different with Islamic militant groups. Neither they nor their international supporters were likely to be responsive to government pressure or Western public opinion. And there was a risk. Public protests can have a perverse effect by driving up ransom demands and complicating negotiations. Worse, they can enhance terrorist propaganda. I learned this the hard way in 2002, when I participated in a global campaign to win the release of Daniel Pearl. The campaign was intended to humanize Pearl, to rally public support, and to isolate the hostage-takers. In the end, this strategy played into the kidnappers' hands by amplifying the visibility of Pearl's eventual murder. Today, Pearl remains among Al Qaeda's most famous victims.

32   The mass public mobilization around hostage-taking in France fuels the global perception that France will respond to hostage blackmail, even though other countries in Europe more readily pay ransom. But the French government is trapped by the dynamic that it created. The public rituals around hostage-taking in France—the mass mobilization, the personal involvement of the French president in resolving the crisis, and, if successful, the triumphant homecoming at Villacoublay air base—have created a challenging political dynamic. While not every hostage-taking sends the French public into the street, once the process is set in motion the government faces tremendous public pressure to bring the hostages home. This is *exactly* what Aubenas wants.

The role of the support committee is to raise the political cost of inaction. "The first interest of the committee is to fight with the government," Aubenas explained. "If the government says, 'This is not good for us, please don't do it,' I say, 'I don't care.' Meanwhile, the family says, 'It's not us, it's the committee.'"

When Aubenas is heading up a support committee, she organizes an action every few weeks. It could be a public rally, a concert, or an art exhibition. The idea is to generate media coverage. When a journalist is involved, she often works closely with Reporters Without Borders. The group advocates for the protection of journalists worldwide and has tremendous visibility in France. She meets regularly with senior government officials, including the president. The families and even the employers of the victims need to maintain a positive and constructive relationship with officials during the hostage ordeal, because cooperation and trust are essential. But Aubenas feels free to give those officials a hard time.

During an active kidnapping, families, friends, and employers are often told by government officials and security experts to keep quiet and avoid the media. The logic is that publicity leads to increased ransom demands. While she leaves the final decision to the family, Aubenas's strategy is to make *more* noise, not less, in order to put pressure on the government, even if that means ransom demands go up. "Let's say that it is something shocking, like $1 million or more," Aubenas insisted. "It's not a little money. But is it better to let someone die on a video on the internet?"

Recognizing that political imperative, the French government put in place an emergency response structure that makes a sharp delineation between political and criminal cases, according to Laurent Combalbert, a former hostage negotiator with the French National Police, and now the head of a private security firm. If the kidnapping is deemed to be strictly criminal in nature—for example, involving a French businessperson in Mexico—then the case is handled by the French National Police. But if a kidnapping is designated as political, negotiations are handled by a small group that might include the head of intelligence, the presidential chief of staff, and the minister of defense. The president is kept informed and personally approves any deal.

While the French government will always negotiate, it does not always pay. Sometimes the price is just too high. In other cases, the potential impact on French interests might be considered too negative. However, one result of this structure is that every hostage case is highly politicized. If the hostages are freed, the president will greet them at the airport per the ritual established during the Lebanese hostage crisis. Triumphant images will be broadcast across the nation and splashed across

34   front pages. If the hostage is killed, it will be perceived as a personal failure of the president, followed by lawsuits and a public reckoning.

In talking to former hostages, their employers, and French government officials, I heard a variety of schemes about how ransom payments are funded. Dorothée Moisan, a French journalist and author of a book on international kidnapping, reports that ransom payments have been made from a special reserve fund approved by the National Assembly, a claim that has been widely reported and substantiated. I was also told of a standing slush fund, a sort of insurance pool, to which French businesses are asked to contribute. In other instances, employers pay the ransom and are quietly reimbursed; or aid money is diverted; or a third country pays on France's behalf and is compensated in some manner.

The French government has consistently claimed it does not "pay" ransom, and in many cases this appears to be technically true. However, the emphasis on whether a government actually pays the ransom itself is misleading. The real distinction is between countries like France that facilitate ransom payments, and others like the U.S. that seek to discourage or even block them.

For Aubenas, however, the issue of whether to pay ransom transcends politics and goes to the very highest ideals of the French Republic. The willingness to negotiate with terrorists and even to pay ransom represents a commitment to democratic principles, she believes. "For me, you win if you get them out," Aubenas told me. "That's democracy, talking to even your worst enemy. It's crazy not to understand that. The strength is to talk with them."

By responding to the craven indifference to human life on   35
the part of the kidnappers with a resolve to preserve it even at
tremendous cost, Aubenas contends, French society is demonstrating its essential humanity and sending a vital message to
the world that undermines the terrorist propaganda. "Paying a
ransom is a victory, not a defeat," Aubenas insists. She recognizes the ransom sometimes goes to terror groups that carry out
other attacks. But preserving the life of the hostage must be the
state's paramount obligation. Aubenas feels it's her role to make
sure the government never forgets it.

While Florence Aubenas sees a willingness to negotiate and
pay ransom as an affirmation of French democratic ideals, not
everyone I spoke with shared that perspective. Others argue
that the French government's willingness to negotiate with terrorists is a vulnerability, a demonstration of the country's lack
of resolve, and a threat to French national security. Perhaps the
most surprising adherent of this view is Georges Malbrunot,
a correspondent for *Le Figaro*. Surprising because Malbrunot,
along with colleague Christian Chesnot, was kidnapped in Iraq
in August 2004. They were held for four months, and released
just two weeks before Aubenas and Hanoun were nabbed. After
Malbrunot and Chesnot were freed, President Jacques Chirac
declared that the French public did not "know of the size of the
efforts and the overall cost for the nation" of bringing them home.

As with Aubenas and Hanoun, there had been a massive
public mobilization in support of the two kidnapped journalists. Soon after they were taken, their kidnappers issued an
ultimatum. Unless the French government repealed its ban on
wearing headscarves in schools, the hostages would be killed.

36   The French government coordinated a global response calling on prominent Islamic leaders to speak out and denounce the threat. In Paris, crowds poured into the street to demonstrate. Malbrunot credits that rapid response with saving his life.

But he also recalls the impact that it had on his captors. Several had initially proposed releasing the hostages after they determined that the two were bona fide journalists and not spies. But another group, seeing the mass protests in France, now believed that the hostages were too valuable to release without a big ransom. "They discovered the publicity in France, and they really enjoyed it," Malbrunot recalled. "They said, 'You are more famous than your president.' There was a huge mobilization in France; there was a kind of panic. And the ransom got higher and higher."

After months of negotiation, a multi-million-dollar ransom was paid by the Qatari government on behalf of the French. (Malbrunot told me that Qatari Foreign Minister Khalid Bin Mohammed Al Attiyah later acknowledged to him that his country had paid the ransom.) Media reports put the ransom as high as $15 million. Malbrunot believes that the publicity about the ransom payment led directly to the kidnapping of Aubenas and Hanoun, who were abducted two weeks after his release. Aubenas told me her abduction was opportunistic, and that her kidnappers did not even know her nationality when they grabbed her.

Malbrunot believes Qatar is playing a dangerous double game. While Qatar hosts an American air base and has close ties to the West, it is also alleged to have provided direct and indirect financing to Jihadi groups around the world, including Al Qaeda. This is partly a question of ideological and religious alignment among some segment of the Qatari elite, but it's

also a way of extending strategic influence and putting pressure on their regional rivals. By brokering ransom payments for
Western hostages, Qatar is able to channel funding to the Jihadi
networks it supports while simultaneously earning the gratitude of Western governments. Naturally, Qatari officials say
that in taking up the cases of Western hostages they are acting
out of a purely humanitarian impulse.

France's hostage politics fuels bad outcomes, Malbrunot
contends. "France is a specialist in hypermobilization," he
insisted. "It comes from a good feeling but it leads to a not very
good result. A kidnapping is a very exciting story for the press.
It's a sad story, a family story, an intelligence story. You have
all the ingredients. But mobilization creates a kind of industry
of mobilization." Malbrunot specifically cites RSF under Robert
Menard, which he accuses of using public protest around
hostage-taking to increase its own visibility and influence.

Didier Le Bret, a prominent French diplomat and intelligence official who oversaw hostage response in the French
government, also has issues with the French approach, which
greatly complicates negotiations. Public mobilization means it
"takes an extra six months to resolve a kidnapping and costs
you a lot more money," he claimed. What Le Bret detests most is
the French tradition of having the president greet the returning
hostages. "It's a terrible idea that highlights our weakness," Le
Bret said. "Sure these people suffered a terrible ordeal, but that
doesn't make them heroes."

But the political dynamic linking mobilization to negotiation has been difficult to break. After all, the process began as
a government-led effort to rally French society in response to
the kidnappings of French citizens in Lebanon. But it has taken

38   on a life of its own. Advocacy organizations like RSF, the support committees, and popular figures like Aubenas now drive
the popular mobilizations. The media responds, providing gen-
erous coverage, and even working behind the scenes to pressure the government to resolve the case when journalists are
involved.

The French government viewed this situation as tolerable,
so long as the cases were resolved. After all, the more media
attention, the greater the political benefit. But the dynamic
began to shift with the emergence of a new group, Al Qaeda
in the Islamic Maghreb (AQIM), which formed in 2006 with a
pledge to be "a bone in the throat of American and French crusaders." The following year, Nicolas Sarkozy was elected president with a promise to shake up the French establishment and
forge closer ties with the United States. Part of that involved
a reconsideration of the French response to hostage-taking,
including an effort to bring it more in line with the U.S. approach.
At the same time, France was facing a genuine security crisis.
According to data provided by the French Foreign Ministry, the
number of French nationals abducted overseas quintupled from
11 to 59 a year between 2004 and 2008. While there was a debate
about whether French citizens were being targeted as a result of
France's propensity to pay ransom, Sarkozy was committed to a
more aggressive response. When a sixty-one-year-old volunteer aid worker named Pierre Camatte was kidnapped by AQIM
in late 2009, the French government not only refused to pay, it
began to put pressure on other European countries whose capit-
ulations to the kidnappers France claimed were fueling sky-
rocketing ransom demands. In January 2010, French Admiral
Edouard Guillaud complained to General William Ward, head

of the U.S. Africa Command, that Spain "has a track record of paying exorbitant sums in ransom and now the demands of the kidnappers are massively inflated."

A month later, Camatte was freed, following the release of four Al Qaeda militants from a jail in Mali. Sarkozy expressed his personal gratitude to Malian President Amadou Toumani Touré and pledged French support in the fight against terrorism. But the release of the four militants deeply angered a number of North African governments, including Algeria. Indeed, the newly released prisoners quickly rejoined the fight.

The tension between Sarkozy's attempt to refine the French response to hostage-taking and Aubenas's efforts to ensure that the government met what she viewed as its historic commitments coalesced around a single case. In December 2009 Hervé Ghesquière, a veteran war reporter for the French broadcaster France 3, was kidnapped in Afghanistan's Kapisa province along with his cameraman Stéphane Taponier. Sarkozy and other senior officials were furious, alleging that the journalists had acted recklessly by leaving a military embed to carry out independent reporting. In a meeting with Sarkozy, Aubenas pushed back, arguing that the journalists were just doing their jobs, and that any criticism of their conduct could wait until they were freed. While the French government called for a "media blackout," meaning the suppression of any mention in the press of the abduction, Aubenas was determined to use media publicity to apply pressure on the government.

At first, the hostages were cited only by their first names. Eventually, Aubenas, RSF, and the French media rallied around a major public campaign that defied the president, using the journalists' full names and keeping their case in the spotlight. When

40   the journalists were released in June 2011, allegedly in exchange for a huge ransom paid to the Taliban, it was a victory not only for the journalists, but for Aubenas and her efforts to defend the principles of French democracy. Sarkozy's attempt to take a harder line had reached its limits. (I will return to this case in Chapter Four)

When its citizens are held hostage, a government must adopt a posture along a continuum—on one end, you walk away from a threat to kill a hostage, and on the other, you capitulate to it. Where a country lands is a reflection of both its strategic interests and its political culture. In the U.S. and the UK, talking tough to terrorists scores political points. In Spain it doesn't, at least not on an international level. France clearly has global interests, but it also has a political culture that rewards popular mobilization. So long as a portion of the French public is willing to march through the streets to demand the return of hostages, the government's options are limited. Thanks in part to Aubenas, any French leader who refuses to recognize this reality is bound to pay a political price.

The General

When General Félix Sanz Roldán was appointed to head Spain's Centro Nacional de Inteligencia, or CNI, in 2009, he was sixty-four years old and headed toward retirement. But Prime Minister José Luis Rodríguez Zapatero needed a consensus figure to lead the troubled spy agency. Sanz Roldán pledged openness and transparency. He declared that "a secret service does not need to be that secret."

The CNI had been wracked by allegations of fraud and criticized for its failure to prevent the terror attack on Madrid's commuter rail system on March 11, 2004, which left two hundred dead and two thousand injured. The attacks, at least indirectly, had helped bring Zapatero to power.

Spain's conservative incumbent, José María Aznar, was leading in the polls at the time the coordinated attack occurred, only days before elections. Voters punished Aznar for his clumsy attempts to blame the attacks on the ETA, the Basque separatist group, when evidence clearly suggested it was carried

42   out by an Al Qaeda-inspired terror cell. More broadly, they were angry that Aznar had led Spain into the war in Iraq, a military campaign that exposed the country to terrorist violence without advancing Spain's position in the world.

To many Spanish voters, the whole Iraq undertaking showed Aznar's subservience to U.S. interests. His obsequious behavior toward U.S. President George W. Bush reinforced this impression. While Aznar earned a visit to Bush's ranch, the deployment of Spanish troops in Iraq was opposed by 90 percent of the Spanish public. Zapatero waited only one day after taking office to fulfill his campaign promise by ordering the complete withdrawal of all Spanish forces from Iraq.

While Spain retained a symbolic presence in Afghanistan, its participation in the war on terror was over. Bush administration officials were furious. U.S. National Security Advisor Condoleezza Rice told Fox News that terrorists could "draw the wrong lesson from Spain." Donald Rumsfeld got into a screaming match with the Spanish Minister of Defense, denouncing the withdrawal as an act of cowardice that would embolden terrorists.

Needing to bolster his credentials with the Spanish military and repair the relationship with the U.S., Zapatero appointed Sanz Roldán as head of the Estado Mayor, or Defense Staff, the top military post in Spain. Sanz Roldán had a conservative pedigree and the rank-and-file support within the military that Zapatero needed. He also had a longstanding relationship with the U.S. military that would allow him to restore trust.

Five years later, with the CNI in crisis, Zapatero once again turned to the general. With the threat from the Basque separatist conflict fading, the CNI sought to reorient its domestic

intelligence network to focus on Islamist terrorists. What the
government had not anticipated was the external challenge.
Within days of assuming his role, Sanz Roldán was consumed
by two kidnapping crises which hit in quick succession. The
first involved the hijacking of a fishing boat, the *Alakrana*, in the
Indian Ocean. The second was the abduction of three Spanish
aid workers in North Africa by Al Qaeda in the Islamic Maghreb.
The response to these two kidnappings would set in place an
approach to hostage-taking that would endure through Zapatero's term and into the next administration.

On October 2, 2009, Somali pirates spotted the *Alakrana* trawling
the waters about four hundred nautical miles northwest of the
Seychelles. The tuna-fishing boat, registered in the Basque city
of Bermeo, was seeking more productive fishing grounds outside a safety zone patrolled by a joint European operation to
combat piracy. The pirates themselves were operating out of a
"mother ship," which allowed them to extend their reach far from
the Somali coast. Two smaller skiffs carrying thirteen pirates
bristling with Kalashnikovs and rocket-propelled grenade
launchers raced toward the *Alakrana*. With its nets deployed,
the *Alakrana* was a sitting duck; the pirates soon boarded the
ship and took control. The head of the pirate boarders, named
Elias, ordered the ship's captain to cut its fishing nets. When the
captain demurred saying it would take less time to haul them
in, the pirates beat him for his insolence. By late morning, the
Alakrana was proceeding at full speed toward the Somali city of
Harare, where the pirates had their base. Thirty-six crew members were on board, sixteen of them hailing from the Basque
region and the rest from Asia and Africa.

44   Back in Madrid, President Zapatero convened members of his cabinet. Participating were Vice President María Teresa Fernández de la Vega, who handled the security portfolio, along with the Ministers of Foreign Relations, International Cooperation, Defense, and the Environment, which overseas maritime issues. Sanz Roldán was in attendance, along with General Julio Rodríguez, who had replaced Sanz Roldán as head of the Defense Staff. General Rodríguez exercised tactical authority over the Spanish naval vessels patrolling the Indian Ocean as part of a joint European anti-piracy operation dubbed *Atalanta*.

The year before, another fishing boat, the *Playa de Bakio*, had been overrun by Somali pirates. The Spanish government responded, sending a military patrol, and helping to manage ransom negotiations through its ambassador in Kenya. The boat was freed after six days, reportedly for a ransom of $1.2 million.

Historically, the Spanish fishing fleet, one of the largest in Europe, had been dominated by companies based in the Basque country. Basque fishermen had a maritime tradition going back centuries. There is some evidence they were trawling the abundant cod fisheries off Newfoundland long before Columbus discovered America. The Basques also have their own language, culture, and national identity. For decades, a violent separatist group, ETA, had used bombings, kidnappings, and other terror tactics to advance its separatist agenda. But the conflict was winding down. As the Zapatero government sought to advance negotiations toward a definitive deal, the president looked for ways to send a clear and strong message to the people of the region that the Spanish government was committed to defending their interests abroad. There would be no better way to achieve this than to the bring the *Alakrana* and its crew home safely.

Besides, Zapatero had already absorbed the lesson sent by   45
Aznar's stinging loss in the 2004 elections. Using military force
to confront the threat of Islamic terrorism outside of Spain
was not a winning political strategy. Negotiation was the best
way forward. While the French privately complained that the
Spanish capitulated too quickly and paid too much, for Zapatero
there was little advantage in taking a hard line.

The nearest Spanish naval vessel, a frigate called *Canarias*,
was about eight hundred nautical miles from the *Alakrana* when
the abduction occurred. It raced at its top speed toward the captured fishing boat, in the hopes of disabling it before it reached
Somali waters, according to a detailed report published in *El
Pais*. But there was too much ground to make up. However, General Rodríguez and the Spanish forces caught a break when a
small skiff with two pirates on board veered off from the mother
ship and headed west toward the Somali coast.

The captain of the *Canarias* informed Madrid of the opportunity to intercept the skiff. General Rodríguez gave the order
to proceed. Using Zodiacs and helicopters deployed from the
Canarias, Spanish sailors surrounded the small boat. One pirate
was shot when he failed to follow instructions but he was not
badly injured and was given medical treatment on board the
Canarias.

Since the frigate was considered Spanish territory, the
pirates were placed under arrest. The case was referred to the
Spanish National Court, known as Audiencia Nacional. At
2:20 a.m. on October 4, Judge Baltasar Garzón—famous for
his international prosecution of Chilean dictator Augusto
Pinochet—ordered the two pirates brought to Spain to stand
trial. Since the *Canarias* needed to remain in the area to support

46 the *Alakrana*, the two pirates were placed on a French vessel, *La Somme*, which transported them to a military base in Djibouti. From there, the pirates were flown back to Spain.

The detention of the two pirates not only created legal complications; it also complicated the negotiations to free the hostages. The pirates holding the ship, now moored off the coast of Somalia, threatened to murder the crew unless their two comrades were released. They tortured the crew psychologically, through threats and mock executions. But when the negotiator informed the pirate representative that he did not have the authority to free their comrades, the pirates dropped the demand. "It was all a big media stunt," General Rodríguez recalled, when I met him in Madrid in the summer of 2017. "For those looking to recover the ransom, the life of those two pirates didn't matter for a moment."

An agreement was reached after forty-four days of negotiations, and a ransom of approximately $3.5 million was packed into a duffel bag. Once the money was prepared, General Rodriguez was told to stand by. A small plane would fly over the area where the *Alakrana* was being held and airdrop the money. "The only thing I knew was the hour," General Rodríguez recalled. "Our goal was to get as close as we could and have a helicopter at the ready."

As soon as Rodriguez received word that the *Alakrana* had been released and the crew was safe, he gave the go-ahead for an operation to recover the ransom. An attack helicopter quickly located the pirates in a Zodiac with the ransom on board, speeding toward the Somali coast. Because of a directive from President Zapatero to avoid loss of life, the gunship fired only on the motor of the speeding boat, which failed to disable it.

Once the boat reached the coast, the kidnappers jumped out
and mixed in with the local population. Rodríguez aborted the
recovery mission and took no further action.

Back in Spain, President Zapatero congratulated all those
who had worked to free the *Alakrana*. The two Somali pirates who
had been captured—one of whom claimed to be a minor—were
convicted and sentenced to jail. At trial, government attor-
neys claimed the ransom had been paid by the shipping company. But in her verdict, the judge determined that the Spanish
government had in fact paid. Her legal logic was interesting.
Noting that the CNI had invoked national security in refusing
to testify, the judge deduced that such an exemption would
have only been granted if the government had paid, as there
would be no national security implication in denying their
involvement. When asked whether the government had paid,
President Zapatero said vaguely that the government, "had
done what it needed to do." From the president's perspective
the operation had been a success: There had been no loss of life,
and the crew on the *Alakrana* were back home with their families in the Basque Country.

Ten days after the successful recovery of the *Alakrana*, Spain was
plunged into the next hostage crisis, this time in North Africa.
On November 29, 2009, three volunteers with a Barcelona-
based humanitarian organization called Acció Solidaria, Albert
Vilalta Cambra, Alicia Gámez Guerrero, and Roque Pascual
Salazar, were kidnapped in Mauritania while participating in
a caravan bringing supplies to neighboring Senegal. The three
volunteers were traveling in a jeep when they were forced to
the side of the road by several cars full of armed men. They

48   had time to radio ahead to other members of the caravan, but their colleagues were distracted because they were listening to a broadcast of the Barcelona-Madrid football game that they were able to pick up from the Spanish island of Las Palmas, off the African coast. When Vilalta asked the attackers what was happening, they shot him three times in the leg. The kidnappers trundled the hostages into their jeeps. Then they drove them across the desert to their camps in neighboring Mali.

At the time, Catalonia was not quite as restive as it would later become, but the region has a history of fierce independence. Zapatero again recognized the political advantage of highlighting the ability of Spain's central government to defend the interests of Catalans abroad. In addition, the charity for which the hostages worked, Acció Solidaria, had close ties to Zapatero's Socialist Party. Once again, Zapatero told his cabinet he wanted the hostages back, but there would be challenges. AQIM was a ruthless group that had demonstrated a willingness to kill hostages for political purposes. In any case, Spain had no military assets to speak of in the region. If it wanted the hostages back, it would have to pay.

Sanz Roldán took personal charge of the operation. The CNI had little expertise or experience with AQIM, but the agency was eventually able to locate someone in Spain who had familiarity with the group. They brought her into the CNI's offices and laid out a map of the region. She pointed to a route through the desert leading from Mauritania to Mali, which was the base of the AQIM operations. Relying on shared U.S. intelligence, the CNI was able to track the progress of the hostage caravan through the desert as it moved almost precisely along the predicted route.

The CNI's most immediate concern was to find a way to
deliver medical supplies so that Vilalta could get necessary
attention for his wounded leg. As the hostages fled across the
desert, Vilalta's captors performed a rudimentary surgery using
the headlights from one of their jeeps. But Vilalta needed anti-
biotics to avoid infection. The CNI enlisted Mustafa Chafi to
serve as intermediary. Chafi, an aide to Burkina Faso's president Blaise Compaoré, had become a conduit to AQIM leader
Mokhtar Belmokhtar, whose *katiba*, or brigade, had carried out
the kidnapping.

About the only interest that the kidnappers and the CNI
shared was to keep the hostages alive. The CNI sought to exploit
this by setting up a channel through Chafi to deliver medical
supplies. Once some modicum of trust was established, the CNI
was able to deliver less essential items, including a teddy bear
secured from the bed of Alicia Gámez in Barcelona. Word had
reached the CNI agents who were helping to manage the negotiations that Gámez was in terrible emotional shape. The agents
hoped the sudden appearance of the teddy bear in her sleeping
quarters would send a reassuring message that the CNI was on
the case and doing everything in its power to procure her liberty.

The CNI agents repeatedly asked the kidnappers to provide
proof of life, including videos. Partly this was a strategy to reas-
sure the families back in Catalonia. As negotiations proceeded,
Belmokhtar agreed to make an unusual gesture, to release
Gámez after three months in captivity. Her captors said it was
because she had converted to Islam, but it may also have been
that her delicate emotional state made her a difficult hostage
to manage. "She was absolutely terrified," Chafi recalled in an
interview with *El País*, describing the journey across the desert

to freedom. Gámez was so distrustful of Chafi that she tried to escape at one point, running off into the sand dunes. His bodyguards had to retrieve her.

Conversion was a constant focus of the militants. Realizing that their treatment would improve, Pascual and Vilalta also decided to embrace Islam after seven months in captivity. Belmokhtar, a fearsome figure who had lost an eye fighting in Afghanistan, was moved to tears. After their conversion, their food rations increased, they got more water, and their guards treated them with slightly less disdain. But the conversion did not fundamentally change the nature of their relationship with their captors.

The CNI had been making slow progress in hammering out a deal, so Sanz Roldán traveled dozens of times to the region to urge the release of Al Qaeda prisoners that the kidnappers had demanded in exchange for their Spanish hostages.

By August, a deal was struck. In addition to securing the release of an Al Qaeda militant from a Mauritanian jail, millions of dollars in ransom was paid. The money may have been fronted by the government of Burkina Faso and offset by an increase in Spanish development aid. Beyond the ransom, there was the commission allegedly paid to Chafi, and the millions of dollars spent on the operations itself, including assembling a field team of CNI agents in the region, developing a network of contacts, flying senior officials in and out, and even purchasing new Land Rovers and then adding dents and wear so they wouldn't stand out operating in the desert.

The ransom was delivered by Chafi at a ceremony in the Malian desert, attended by fifty AQIM fighters who arrived in eight all-terrain vehicles. They fired their guns in the air and

embraced their new Spanish brothers before turning them over
to Chafi. The hostages were driven across the desert, then flown
by helicopter to Gorom-Gorom, in northern Burkina Faso.
There they were received by CNI agents who provided them
with clean clothes and food, including Iberian ham. Pascual and
Vilalta quickly discarded their new faith and ate the haram food,
downing a few beers. They shaved their beards and donned new
clothes. This was part of the re-integration strategy that the
CNI had developed to quickly give the hostages control over
their lives. On the flight back to Spain, Pascual asked the CNI
agents how much had been paid in ransom. "Don't worry about
that," a CNI agent answered. Newspaper reports alleged it was as
much as $8 million.

Former International Cooperation Minister Soraya Rodríguez, now an opposition member of Congress, justified Spanish
government policy of handling complex negotiations and providing support for the families. "I was personally in charge of
the relationship with the families and this is an area where
I think we did a good job," Rodriguez explained. During the
hostage crisis, she made daily phone calls to the families, trying
to give them hope. But she was always truthful. The trust established, Rodríguez believes, helped convince the families not
to go to the media, and not to succumb to the fraudsters and
opportunists who called claiming they were in touch with the
kidnappers.

"The families simply don't have the means to resolve a kidnapping by themselves," Rodríguez argued. "Only the state has
them. Even if the family has the money and they want to pay,
they don't have a way to get the money to the hostage-takers or
to find an adequate intermediary."

52   The efforts to end two successive crises would define an
approach of hostage-taking that endured through the Zapatero
administration. In 2011—buffeted by the Euro crisis and a near
collapse of the Spanish economy—voters returned the conservatives to power. But the hostage policy under the government
of Mariano Rajoy remained unchanged. It's a policy of negotiation and restraint that places a maximum emphasis of the safe
return of the hostages. The French government actively denies
paying ransom, but Spain uses more ambivalent language.
When Rajoy's Foreign Minister was asked in 2012 whether his
government had paid to secure release of two aid workers kidnapped in Africa the year before, he responded, "The government did what it had to do"—the same phrase Zapatero had
used in 2009. The non-denial denial is a way for the Spanish
government to take credit for the successful outcome.

If your goal is to bring the hostages home, paying ransom
works. Every one of the estimated seventy Spaniards taken hostage by Islamist groups and Somali pirates have come home
alive. This record is unmatched by any other country.

On the whole, the Spanish public and the media support the
government's efforts. When citizens are taken hostage in Spain
there are no committees, no banners hung from buildings, and
no street protests. As the wife of one former hostage pointed
out, there is no need to protest if you are confident the government is already doing all it can.

The Spanish media goes along as well. "When there is a kidnapping, the government asks for discretion and the press acts
responsibly," explained José María Irujo, who covers the intelligence beat for *El País*. "No newspapers have broken the pact,
which has the support of everyone, from the owners to the

reporters. We could scoop each other, but what value does a   53
scoop have if you put someone's life in danger?" Sanz Roldán
points with satisfaction to a column published in 2015 by José
Apezarena, the editor of an online news portal, El Confidencial
Digital. The headline reads, "Silence, the CNI Is Working."

"The government has decided to put above all the life of
the individual," Irujo argued. "Spanish society is not prepared
to accept that our citizens will die for a principle. The government will pay. The political cost of letting someone die would be
enormous. The government would be perceived as not having a
heart. I can't imagine living in a society like that, a society that
is so distant and cold."

The benefits of the Spanish approach are obvious. The hostages come home. The costs are more difficult to assess.

One of the most frequent arguments against the payment
of ransom is that it encourages further kidnapping. This correlation appears so obvious that it has been taken as an article
of faith among governments that have adopted a no concessions
policy. But the research is far from conclusive.

In the early 1970s, in response to a series of kidnappings
targeting American diplomats in Latin America, the Santa
Monica-based RAND Corporation carried out research to
assess the effectiveness of a no concessions policy. In the end
the RAND researchers were "unable to find persuasive evidence
supporting the assertion that a no concessions policy provided an effective deterrent" against future kidnappings. More
recent research confirmed this initial finding. A 2015 study by
the Combating Terrorism Center at West Point found no correlation between the hostage policy of a particular country and
the likelihood that its nationals would be targeted. "Although

54   kidnappings are often thought of as preplanned events against specific individuals, they often seem to occur opportunistically against individuals who are in the wrong place at the wrong time," the report noted. A 2017 New America Foundation study reached a similar conclusion. It analyzed data of 1,185 Westerners from 32 countries kidnapped since 2001 by terrorist, militant, and pirate groups, and concluded that "there is no clear link between a nation's ransom policy and the number of citizens taken hostage." Instead, it found that kidnapping is driven by "conditions of general instability," meaning war and lawlessness.

A 2016 study entitled "Why Concessions Should Not Be Made to Terrorist Kidnappers" and published in the *European Journal of Political Economy* used a different set of data and reached a very different conclusion. Applying sophisticated quantitative analysis, the authors concluded that making concessions does increase the likelihood of future kidnappings by between 64 and 87 percent. The authors claim their data includes more information regarding negotiations and ransom payments. However, that data is drawn from media sources, which based on my own reporting and research, can be unreliable on such matters. The study also failed to take into the account the relative "supply" of Western hostages. In others words, the fact that Europeans rather than Americans are kidnapped in North Africa may have nothing to with differences in concessions policy and everything to do with the fact that there are simply more Europeans present.

While the available data is inconclusive on whether a policy of no concessions leads to fewer future kidnappings, it is solid on another point: Countries that pay ransom tend to get their hostages home alive. "Eighty-one percent of European Union hostages held by Jihadi terrorist groups were freed," the New America study noted. Meanwhile, hostages from the U.S. and the UK, both of which refuse to pay ransom, were freed 25 and 33 percent of the time, respectively.

Anecdotally, European journalists who operate in conflict zones told me they do not believe that kidnap victims are targeted based on nationality, and therefore feel safer rather than more vulnerable knowing their governments are prepared to negotiate for their release. Others, like American journalist Graeme Wood, who has reported extensively on the Islamic State, take a different view. They argue that the European policy of paying ransom puts all journalists and aid workers at risk. "As an unkidnapped journalist with no living colleagues I know of in captivity, I can say that making huge payments to terrorist groups, as Western governments have done in recent years, has been disastrous," Wood wrote in *The New York Review of Books*.

While the studies I cited indicate that most kidnappings are opportunistic and not based on nationality, this may not be true in every case. U.S. government sources with access to intelligence reports told me that AQIM leaders spoke of targeting Europeans because of their propensity to pay. Only a handful of the U.S. and British hostages were taken by AQIM. One of them, Edwin Dyer, was beheaded in 2009 after the British government flatly refused to pay a ransom.

While the correlation between ransom payment and targeted kidnappings is debated, no one denies that the money paid to terror groups is used for terrible purposes. Ransom has become a significant source of financing for military operations and criminal enterprises carried out by Jihadi groups around the world.

56   In Afghanistan, the Taliban claimed they used the $10 million ransom paid for the return of twenty-one Korean missionaries in 2007 to underwrite a major military offensive targeting European and American security forces operating in the country. In the case of AQIM, ransom money helped the group develop into a significant military force and a threat to regional stability.

This is why the loudest and most consistent objection to European ransom payments often comes from local governments affected by such policies. In 2007, Afghanistan's President Hamid Karzai succumbed to pressure from the Italian government and released five Taliban prisoners in exchange for the liberty of kidnapped journalist Daniele Mastrogiacomo. Karzai then went on television to declare that he would never negotiate again. The Taliban responded by beheading Mastrogiacomo's Afghan news assistant. The Algerian government, which has been targeted in terror attacks carried out by AQIM, has repeatedly called on European governments to end their practice of paying ransom.

Ransom money has also been used to finance Al Qaeda's global operations. Osama bin Laden was known to be personally involved in negotiations and in setting strategy. In 2011, he advised AQIM to kill the hostage with "the lowest rank." Nasser al-Wuhayshi, the leader of Al Qaeda in the Arabian Peninsula, wrote in a 2012 letter to Belmokhtar that, "Kidnapping hostages is an easy spoil which I may describe as a profitable trade and a precious treasure." Later, Al Qaeda leaders excoriated Belmokhtar for only obtaining $1 million for Canadian diplomats Robert Fowler and Louis Guay, according to a letter obtained by journalist Rukmini Callimachi. (That deal was also brokered by Chafi, the advisor to the Burkina Faso's

president, according to Fowler's book.) The U.S. government
estimated that ransom paid by European governments to terrorists between 2008 and 2014 totaled more than $165 million.
A *New York Times* analysis put the number at $125 million over
the same period. (A senior U.S. official told me in December
2017 that the updated figure was closer to $300 million.)

AQIM used the proceeds from ransom payments to expand
and diversify its operations in ways that directly threatened
European security. The group—along with more criminally
minded gangs operating in the Sahara—expanded its smuggling
operations using existing routes to move cocaine obtained from
Colombia's FARC guerrillas into Europe. They also branched
out into human trafficking, in later years moving desperate
migrants from Sub-Saharan Africa through the deserts and
onto flimsy rafts launched into the Mediterranean in the hopes
of being picked up by a European patrol.

"These roads have always been used to move cigarettes,
weapons, and cocaine coming from Colombia into Europe," said
Alain Juillet, a former senior official in France's DGSE and now
a private security analyst. "Today, the same people are involved
and are dealing in migrants. Criminals and terrorists are making
money on the back of migrants, fueling more terrorism."

For Vicki Huddleston, who served as U.S. Ambassador to
Mali and later as Deputy Assistant Secretary of Defense for
African Affairs, the willingness to pay ransom on the part of
European governments strengthens terror and criminal networks and undermines regional security. In several instances,
she saw European aid money diverted to fund ransom payments, an approach that she believes fuels local corruption and weakens trust. "The Europeans have a lot to answer

58 for," Huddleston told *The New York Times.* "It's a completely two-faced policy."

European officials and analysts I spoke with pushed back against this characterization. Ransom payments finance terror groups, but so does international drug trafficking, the global arms trade, and the misappropriation of aid payments, all areas where poorly conceived or executed U.S. policies play a role. "It seems the United States wants to cast itself as the good guy, and Europe as the bad guy," Spain's General Rodríguez told me. "I'd be very careful comparing numbers, like the amount that Europe has paid in ransom with the sale of weapons to Saudi Arabia and other countries which are suspected of having ties to terrorism."

By refusing to negotiate, the U.S., the UK, and other governments that favor no concessions are also missing out on opportunities to exploit kidnapping negotiations to secure intelligence that can be used to recover the ransom or target the individuals or organizations involved. Didier Le Bret told me that France relied on intelligence gathered from hostage negotiations in planning and carrying out its military campaign in Mali, following the AQIM takeover of Timbuktu in late 2012. Two separate European officials told me that they had tracked and recovered ransoms after they were paid.

Terrorism experts I spoke with also say there is little evidence that withholding ransom payments actually leads to a decline in kidnapping. What reduces kidnapping is resolving conflict, increasing security, or in some cases destroying the organization carrying out the attacks. Hostage-taking was a central feature of the conflicts in Lebanon and Colombia but declined as those conflicts wound down. It was common in

Peru until radical organizations like MRTA and Sendero Luminoso were wiped out. Meanwhile, increased military patrols in
the Indian Ocean combined with enhanced security measures
implementing by shipping companies has reduced the threat of
Somali piracy.

Some experts believe those gains are temporary because
the conditions that led Somalis to get into the hostage business—poverty, lawlessness, and festering resentments about
depletion of their fisheries—remain unchanged. "I think the
main reason piracy declined was that that local people rebelled
against the pirates," London-based Somali journalist Jamal
Osman told me. "The legitimacy that the pirates had earned
by casting their actions as just retribution for the plundering
of the Somali fisheries by large European trawlers was squan-
dered when newly wealthy pirates began using drugs, drinking
alcohol, and abusing local women. Somalia is a violent place,
but it's also a conservative place. People are still saying, 'they
are stealing our resources and we should do something about
this.' The warships that people see off the coast are watching
the pirates. People say, 'why can't they stop the bad guys who are
entering our waters and emptying our seas?'"

With its low-slung concrete buildings and manicured lawns,
the CNI headquarters on the outskirts of Madrid looks like a
Los Angeles office park. Sanz Roldán's vast corner office is dec-
orated with mementos and maps and a few cherished posses-
sions, including a photograph of Charlize Theron. For years
Sanz Roldán would arrive each morning and ask his secretary
if he had gotten any calls from the South African actress, who
had become a bit of an obsession. His staff decided that for the

60   general's birthday they would actually get the actress to call. But the "operation" was unsuccessful. Theron did, however, send a signed publicity shot.

In person, Sanz Roldán combines self-deprecating humor with Old World charm. For someone who is Spain's top spy, he likes to talk, and he waved off aides who wandered into the room to tell him it was time for his next appointment. But when I asked Sanz Roldán to discuss Spain's approach to hostage-taking he did not answer directly. "No government will ever admit it negotiates with terrorists or pays ransom," Sanz Roldán pointed out.

There are ethical, moral, and security-related issues that determine the response in any international kidnapping. But the decision is fundamentally and appropriately political, Sanz Roldán believes. While no concessions countries seek to depo-liticize decision making by putting in place a policy frame-work, Spain expects the president to determine the response based on the specific circumstances. The role of the CNI is to use its analysis and intelligence assets to ensure the president has the information to make the best possible decision. In 2011, this relationship was formalized. The CNI was restructured and removed from the Ministry of Defense. Henceforth, Sanz Roldán would have a direct line to the president. In 2014, Rajoy reappointed the general to a second five-year term. There are no competing intelligence agencies in Spain, and the CNI handles both internal and external functions. "I have no problem coor-dinating with myself," he points out. Once a decision is made by the president, it's the CNI's responsibility to execute it.

Spain's national crisis center is located in a separate building on the CNI campus. The enormous round room is empty when I am invited to stop by. But when Spain confronts an emergency, the dozens of terminals arrayed along curving rows and facing a giant arched screen blink and buzz. The president and his senior advisor sit at the head of the large conference table in the middle of the action. When the President is not present, Sanz Roldán is often the senior official in charge.

At the back of the room is a small collection of photos featuring Spanish hostages. Here is the *Playa de Bakio* being escorted by a military frigate. Here are Pascual and Vilalta sitting at the feet of their armed captors shortly after being kidnapped. Here is aid worker Ainhoa Fernández de Rincon being handed over to CNI agents in Mali in July, 2012. Here are journalists Javier Espinosa and Ricardo García Vilanova arriving at the Torrejon de Ardoz military base, after being freed by the Islamic State in March, 2014. Not one of these hostages was rescued. Not one escaped. The cost of their freedom was millions of euros given to militants and criminals.

Sanz Roldán appreciates the moral challenges, but is clearly gratified by the success of the CNI's efforts. Each year, he receives a Christmas card from one former hostage he helped free. It reads: "Thanks to you, I am celebrating Christmas this year." Says the general: "This is the only recognition that I need for a job well done."

The Insurance Broker

In 1982, a British insurance broker named Doug Milne set out in search of new markets. His specialty was kidnapping and ransom insurance, known in the industry as K & R. Naturally, he was looking at places around the world where people were being nabbed. One such place was Colombia.

Milne enrolled in a Spanish-language course in London and a month later, with rudimentary skills and only one or two solid contacts on the ground, he boarded a flight to Bogotá. On his first day in the city, Milne was walking to a meeting with a potential client from Japan when "a guy pulled up alongside and this chap who was walking in front of me, his head just exploded." It was a drive-by assassination.

Milne canceled the meeting and spent the afternoon in the Trafalgar Bar near Bogotá's entertainment district. "I missed my meeting and I think I left there about eleven o'clock at night after having drunk a couple of flagons of Tres Esquinas rum," Milne recalled.

Of course, Milne was horrified. But he also realized that
he'd come to the right place. While he knew nothing about the
victim or the motive, the murder drove home to him the extent
to which Colombian society was at the mercy of criminals and
guerrilla. His clients needed what he had to offer.

Kidnapping and ransom insurance was first created in
response to the Lindbergh baby kidnapping but didn't really
catch on until the 1960s, following a spate of kidnappings in
Europe. These were carried out by criminals and political groups
using terror tactics, like ETA in Spain, the Red Army Faction in
Germany and the Red Brigades in Italy. The specialized insurance initially catered to wealthy individuals and was later mar-
keted to companies to cover their employees. The appeal was
simple: In the event of a kidnapping, the insurance would provide reimbursement for a ransom payment.

There were caveats and carve outs to prevent fraud and
ensure the existence of the policy did not increase the risk of
kidnapping. The first was that the policy had to be kept secret.
In fact, it could be voided if its existence became public. The
concern was that if the kidnappers became aware of the policy,
they would demand more money. Companies that have this type
of insurance generally do not tell their employees. Insured families keep the information closely guarded.

The second principle is that the policy will only reimburse
the ransom once it is paid. The insurance company never fronts
any money. In order to raise the cash, the victim's family will
probably have to liquidate assets—mortgage the house, sell
stocks, pool money from other relatives. This process makes
the negotiations credible by dragging them out. This is not

64   just about minimizing the payout by the insurance company. Quickly making good on a large ransom raises the expectations of future kidnappers. It can make hostage-taking more lucrative and inevitably more common. It also increases the risk of a "double dip," in which the kidnappers become convinced that their initial ransom demand was too low. They then refuse to release the victim until a second ransom is paid.

In the 1960s and 1970s, when K & R insurance first came on the market, the policyholders were left on their own to negotiate the ransom and work out details and logistics with the kidnappers. But over time it became clear that this approach had serious disadvantages. The families were obviously under tremendous stress and generally had no experience handling such tense high-stakes negotiations. They were certainly not in a position to strike the best deal. This would mean greater hardship for the victim and a bigger payout for the insurance companies.

In the mid-1970s, Julian Radcliffe, an insurance broker with Hogg Robinson, came up with an idea that would revolutionize the industry. Milne describes Radcliffe as "a very clever man, a very creative man, a bit of a genius, actually." Radcliffe and several colleagues convinced Hogg Robinson to set up a subsidiary focused on hostage response. They called it Control Risks. Control Risks would hire security experts to handle negotiations. These would be people with expertise, mostly former military and police. The cost of hiring the consultant was included in the policy and borne by the insurance company. In 1982, Control Risks became an independent company.

This was the product that Milne was peddling back in the late 1970s when he began to explore the world for new opportunities. At the time, the threat of kidnapping was declining

in Europe as the radical, leftist groups that had used the tactic
either faded away or were busted up. The market was fairly small
and specialized, but included wealthy families in Spain's Basque
region. Some of them had investments in Latin America and
wanted to know if their policies would cover them if they were
kidnapped in the region (the answer was yes). By the early 1980s,
hostage-taking was exploding in Latin America, particularly in
Colombia. Surely, there would be wealthy families interested in
purchasing insurance.

When Milne arrived in Colombia, kidnappings were being
carried out by common criminals, drug cartels, and leftist
guerrillas, including the National Army of Liberation (ELN),
and the Revolutionary Armed Forces of Colombia (FARC). Both
groups espoused a Marxist ideology but had different origins,
grievances, and zones of operations. One area of agreement
was that kidnapping was a legitimate tactic of war. Ransom
was a reallocation of Colombia's highly skewed wealth, and
hostages could also be held to extract political concessions.
The vast majority of the thousands of kidnapping victims were
Colombians, but wealthy foreigners were also targets. In the
late 1990s, FARC instituted a practice that became known as
the *pesca milagrosa*, a reference to Jesus's Miracle of the Fishes,
but also the name of a popular children's game in Colombia.
The guerrillas would set up roadblocks, checking the identifi-
cation of everyone they stopped against a list of targets. Those
on it were immediately detained.

Milne soon discovered a vast, untapped market. As an
insurance broker, he sold a variety of policies offered by different
companies available through the Lloyds exchange in London.
The job of the broker is to serve the client and to advocate for

66   their interests in the event of a claim. The underwriters represent the insurance companies. Specialized, high-risk policies were placed on the Lloyds insurance exchange, and Milne would field offers from different underwriters. He would select the policy that best suited his client.

Milne's parents were in the oil business and he grew up in the Middle East. He attended boarding school in Scotland, and only got into the insurance business after "failing as an artist." He combines British reserve with an easy laugh. He dresses in tailored suits with a perfectly positioned pocket square. He enjoys a good stiff drink, sometimes two. To his South American clients, he was as quintessentially British as James Bond. "When I went to Colombia everyone wanted to see me," Milne recalled. "I started with a few contacts, but it grew like topsy. All their friends at the golf club wanted to meet. We got enough business to recruit a team in London. We started specializing. It suddenly became a viable business."

Milne rented a house in downtown Bogotá, which he made a base for his travels throughout Latin America, from Guatemala to Brazil. By the time he wrapped up his stint in Latin America ten years later, he had sold hundreds of new policies, recruited a specialized team in London focusing on the Latin America market, and developed a new service to provide risk mitigation. Insurance companies and their clients both have an interest in reducing the likelihood of a kidnapping. So Milne came up with a new "preventative training" program that educated clients on risk avoidance and crisis response. He then convinced insurance companies that they should foot the bill. Today, Milne's company, Special Contingency Risks, is a subsidiary of Miller insurance brokers, which in turn is part of Willis Towers

Watson. The SCR crisis center is located in a farmhouse outside London.

The K & R insurance business has grown up as well. Today two insurers—Hiscox in the UK and AIG in the U.S.—dominate the market. About a half dozen additional companies that issue K & R policies are listed on the Lloyds exchange in London. There are also many security firms that specialize in kidnap response, from large corporate entities like GardaWorld and Kroll, to small, boutique concerns, including one-person operations, scattered throughout Europe and the United States.

Hostage negotiation has become something of an industry, with conferences, conventions, and shared strategies. In general, the negotiators operate in the background, and try to convince the kidnappers that the family or the business has limited resources. Ransoms paid to criminal groups are generally between 5 and 10 percent of the initial ask. More than 97 percent of kidnappings handled by professional negotiators are successfully resolved through the payment of ransom, according to several different security consultants with access to internal industry data. A small percentage of hostages escape and a very few are rescued through high-risk operations. Less than 1 percent are killed. More than 75 percent of Fortune 500 companies have K&R insurance policies and the overall market is between $250 and $300 million a year.

International hostage negotiation is high stakes, but the industry's professionals shun drama and manage each situation like a business transaction. They have refined the process to the point that negotiators can now predict with a good degree of accuracy how long a case will take to resolve and how much ransom will be paid based on the location of the incident and the

68   nationality of the victim. Often, the haggling over the amount of the ransom is typical of a commercial transaction, except that lives are on the line. Some critics argue that this tendency to look for monetary settlements fuels global kidnapping. Others simply find it unseemly that the companies, which charge hefty fees for their services, are making a comfortable profit off of human suffering,

Milne prides himself on the personal touch he provides to his clients, including serving as the initial contact when kidnapping occurs. He also makes it a point to monitor the work of the negotiators, and to urge clients to replace those who in his view are not up to snuff. The security consultants, with backgrounds in the military or law enforcement, are a gruff bunch who don't always appreciate having someone looking over their shoulder. While Milne is a leading figure in the K & R world, there are many others. Some grumble that in an industry that values discretion, Milne is a bit of self-promoter. But no one denies his success. While Milne has faced some difficult moments—one of his clients in Colombia was cut into tiny pieces for daring to report his kidnapping to the police—the vast majority of the approximately eighty cases Milne handles each year "go to plan," meaning the hostages are released. "If kidnappers are not making it on the money front, they will start making political demands, or sell their hostages to terrorists," Milne argued. "It's much better to resolve them as commercial cases."

London is the global center for K & R insurance. It's also the base for many of the world's leading security firms. But it has not always been a comfortable fit. This is because the UK has been a leader of the no concessions camp. Margaret Thatcher, who became Prime Minister in 1979, talked a tough game, repeatedly emphasizing that Britain does not negotiate with terrorists, pay ransom, or make concessions. She was not happy that London had become the center of a global industry that did just that.

In April 1986, Jennifer Guinness, the wife of banker and member of the Guinness brewing family John Guinness, was kidnapped by the Provisional IRA, which demanded a ransom of $2.6 million. She was rescued in a police raid only eight days after being abducted. But the fact that a K & R policy had been triggered and the security firm Control Risks brought on to negotiate a possible ransom fueled outrage. "Private security firms such as the ones called in on the Guinness kidnapping are operating at the very frontiers of official tolerance," a top police official announced.

The Thatcher government charged that the insurance industry was fueling a global kidnapping epidemic, facilitating the payment of ransom, and undermining the British no concessions policy. In 1986, the issue was debated in Parliament, which passed a motion expressing concern. There was even talk of working through European institutions to impose a ban on K & R insurance throughout the European Union.

Recognizing that its very existence was under threat, the security industry rallied. "There was a study done that argued the case that if you were insured you were actually less likely to be kidnapped," Milne recalled. "The more aware of the risk, the more you do to avoid being a target." The industry claimed that since the policies were kept secret, it was clear that people were not being kidnapped because they had insurance. Rather, they were being taken hostage because they had resources. Banning insurance would not change the dynamic. Since the

70   policies only provided reimbursement and were always written for amounts less than the net worth of the policyholder, the industry also argued that insurance did not drive up the amount of payment. What's more, security consultants who handled the negotiations often came from a law enforcement background and cooperated with authorities to bring the perpetrators to justice. And they pointed out that the availability of K & R insurance helped international businesses to manage risk, which in turn allowed companies—including British and European companies—to operate in dangerous environments while exercising appropriate "duty of care" toward their employees.

The public debate helped the insurance industry to refine its arguments and lobbying skills, which would serve it well throughout the next decade. While the British and European debate eventually wound down without new legislation or regulatory measures being put in place, individual countries in Europe and throughout the world continued to wrestle with how best to respond to the crime of kidnapping. Italy, for example, passed a law in 1991 that banned the payment of ransom and the sale of K & R insurance. It froze the assets of the victim's family and made it illegal to provide assistance, meaning professional negotiators could be criminally prosecuted. Italians, who continued to be victimized, simply stopped reporting the crimes to the authorities. Victims would arrange to pay the ransom outside the country, for example in neighboring Switzerland. Meanwhile, Colombia banned ransom payments, then unbanned them, then banned them again. Reports of massive payments, like the more than $20 million ransom allegedly paid to win the freedom of Mexican banker Alfredo Harp Helú in 1994, fueled public debate. Through it all, the K & R industry

not only survived but thrived. By 2000, more than 60 percent
of Fortune 500 companies carried K & R insurance for corporate employees.

Then came September 11, 2001.

The terror attacks, and the wave of high profile kidnappings
carried out by Al Qaeda-aligned groups, spawned a coordinated,
global effort to deprive terror groups of financing. Since kidnapping for ransom was one source of revenue, this changed the
terms of the debate. Rather than challenging the K & R industry
as a whole, governments sought to draw a clearer distinction
between criminal groups, to whom ransom could legally be paid,
and terror groups, to whom it could not. The U.S. and UK governments both maintained lists of Foreign Terrorist Organizations who could not receive ransom payments. In industry
parlance, these groups were designated as "proscribed."

When applied to real-life kidnappings, the attempt to draw
distinctions between criminal and terrorist organizations created tremendous complexities that were difficult to manage. It
was clear that K & R policies could not reimburse policyholders
who paid a ransom to a terrorist group. But could security consultants legally assist families or businesses who sought to
make such a payment? Could they handle negotiations and
help to deliver the money? Could they help families to raise and
assemble the funds? And what about the families themselves?
Would they be held legally liable for paying ransom to terrorists? "It's all a gray area," Milne acknowledged.

Further complicating the process is the fact that kidnappers
often try to hide their identity. Hostage negotiators told me that
some terror groups pretend to be criminal organizations so they
can collect ransoms. The opposite also occurs. Criminal groups

72   who are ignorant of the legal prohibitions sometimes pretend to be terror organizations in the hopes that the fearsome reputation of these groups will push negotiations along. Under the law, the onus is on the insurance company to demonstrate that kidnappers are "proscribed" in order to invalidate the policy. Negotiators working for the victim's family would sometimes refrain from asking obvious questions about the group holding the hostage. They simply preferred not to know.

Meanwhile, determinations about which groups were put on government lists of terrorist groups were often politically determined and sometimes arbitrary. For example, Mexican drug cartels were considered criminal. It was perfectly legal to pay them ransom even though they functioned more like terror organizations. The cartels engaged in wholesale violence, filming murders and posting them to YouTube with the objective of sowing terror and threatening regional and global stability through their criminal and trafficking networks.

A 2011 case, Masefield AG vs. Amlin Corporate Member, determined that the payment of ransom to Somali pirates was legal under British law. As a result, Somali pirates were presumed to be criminals rather than terrorists, even when ties to the Al Shabab militants were alleged. Meanwhile, it was illegal to pay ransom to a criminally oriented kidnapping cell in Nigeria if they were seen to have ties to proscribed groups like Boko Haram.

Milne, who began his career insuring wealthy Colombian clients against kidnapping by leftist guerrillas, admits that once FARC was added to the proscribed list in 1997, his clients were "out of luck." Since criminals sometimes carried out kidnappings and then sold hostages to terror groups, paying ransom could be legal one day and illegal the next. In the age of terror, the intersection of disparate national policies and the insurance market creates inequalities and complexities that determine who lives and who dies in international kidnapping cases.

In my research, I've found there are essentially three variables. Does the hostage have kidnapping and ransom insurance? Was he or she kidnapped by a criminal group? Is the victim a national of a country that pays ransom? Those with the best chance of survival can answer "yes" to all three questions. Those who answer "no" to one or more have few good options. They can either wait for a rescue, try to escape, or hope their family can find a way to deliver a ransom despite the legal prohibitions.

Kristen Mulvihill confronted this bleak landscape after her husband, *New York Times* reporter David Rohde, was kidnapped in Afghanistan in November, 2008, along with an Afghan assistant, Tahir Luddin, and their driver. The three were smuggled across the border into Pakistan, where they were held by the Haqqani network, a militant group with links to both Al Qaeda and Pakistan's intelligence service, known as the ISI. Mulvihill had access to security consultants, the full support of the *Times,* and regular contact with senior U.S. officials.

Despite this, the negotiations were a welter of confusion with multiple channels of communication; cascading demands from the kidnappers involving both money and the release of Taliban prisoners; two teams of security consultants; and multiple U.S. government agencies involved, from the FBI to the State Department. Mulvihill obviously recognized the Haqqani network was doing "bad things" and did not want to be accused of funding terrorism. But she was still prepared to negotiate. The FBI made clear that the government had never prosecuted

74   a family for paying ransom and that she would not face legal jeopardy for doing so. "I was told that early on and throughout," Mulvihill recalled.

Soon after her husband was kidnapped, Mulvihill enlisted the support of Richard Holbrooke, the legendary U.S. diplomat who had helped secure Rohde's release after he was taken hostage by a pro-Serbian militia while reporting in Bosnia in 1995. In his new role as President Obama's Special Envoy for Afghanistan and Pakistan, Holbrooke had taken a personal interest in Rohde's case and had raised concerns with Pakistani intelligence officials. Holbrooke's efforts didn't win Rohde's freedom. But the ISI, at least in Mulvihill's view, was able to use its influence with the Haqqani network to ensure better treatment for Rohde. In March, 2009, Holbrooke called Mulvihill to let her know he had done all he could. "We can't do a raid," she remembered him saying. "The diplomatic approach isn't working. If it were me—I'm telling you as a private citizen—one million, two million, what does it matter? It's a human life."

Mulvihill was furious because she saw Holbrooke as signaling the limits of U.S. involvement, effectively letting her know that if she prepared to pay ransom she would be on her own. The advice was also unhelpful to the extent that no serious ransom negotiations were underway. Later, she came to appreciate Holbrooke's honesty.

In kidnapping cases, time can be your enemy or your friend. In Rohde's case, it worked to his advantage. Over the months of his captivity, Rohde has been able to build enough trust with his captors to move freely around the compound where he was being held. Slowly, he developed an escape plan. He found a rope, which he stashed outside a bathroom ledge, and one night

he and Tahir Luddin snuck past sleeping guards and used the
rope to lower themselves off a twenty-foot-high wall. They
hobbled down a dry riverbed to reach a Pakistani military base.
After some tense negotiations with frightened guards, they
were eventually allowed to enter. Rohde called his family from a
borrowed cell phone to let them know he was free.

A year earlier, Canadian journalist Amanda Lindhout had
been kidnapped in Somalia, along with an Australian colleague,
Nigel Brennan. As young freelancers, they did not have insurance. Officially, neither Canada nor Australia pay ransom.
Driven by desperation, their families found a way forward.

The one factor in their favor was that the group that kidnapped the two journalists was a criminal and not a terror organization. They justified their actions in religious terms, but
they also acknowledged to their hostages that they were after
money. Because they were not "terrorists," the Canadian government entered into negotiations, offering to build a school
or provide development aid in exchange for Lindhout's release.
But the kidnappers wanted cash. They tortured Lindhout to put
more pressure on her family, which had few resources. Realizing the negotiations were going nowhere, Lindhout's mother,
Lorinda Stewart, decided the only hope was to pay a ransom.
Canadian officials had warned Stewart that paying ransom was
against the law and that she could be prosecuted for doing so.
But Stewart forged ahead.

Once Stewart made the decision, the Royal Canadian
Mounted Police, which had been handling the case, withdrew all
support. The hostage negotiating team that had been camped in
her living room moved out. Stewart, working with the Brennan
family in Australia, eventually raised enough money to hire a

76   security consultant from London-based firm AKE to take over the
      negotiations. The consultant advised the Lindhout and Brennan
      families that negotiations would take several months and that
      they would have to pay a ransom of around $600,000 each. His
      prediction was spot on. Lindhout and Brennan were freed in
      November 2009. Their families ended up in massive debt.

      A number of U.S. and British hostages have also been res-
      cued. On January 25, 2012, President Obama entered Congress
      to deliver his State of the Union speech. Cameras caught him
      telling Defense Secretary Leon Panetta "good job tonight" and
      giving him a vigorous pat on the back. Although it had not yet
      been announced, earlier that evening, Navy Seals had dropped
      into Somalia and rescued kidnapped U.S. aid worker Jessica
      Buchanan and her Danish colleague Poul Thisted, shooting
      dead nine of their kidnappers. Buchanan and Thisted had been
      abducted the previous October. Officials had decided to launch
      a rescue because Buchanan had developed a kidney infection,
      and they believed her life was in danger. Negotiations, which
      were being carried out by a security consultant and monitored
      by the FBI, were not progressing fast enough. The kidnappers
      had initially demanded $10 million, and had recently rejected
      a $1 million offer. Most importantly, the U.S. had good intelli-
      gence on the hostages' location and ideal weather conditions
      for a successful rescue.

      The Buchanan rescue effort was emotionally satisfying.
      But rescuing hostages through military force is not a scalable
      solution to international hostage-taking. First, only a handful
      of countries have the military ability to pull off such a raid. The
      deterrent value of rescue attempts is also difficult to judge or
      quantify. Less than a week before the Buchanan raid, freelance

journalist Michael Scott Moore was nabbed while reporting on Somali pirates. "The Buchanan raid happened right after Michael was picked up and the pirates were furious about it," recalled a source close to the case. "We thought the reason the initial ransom demand was so high was because the kidnappers had just been burned by the U.S. That may have accounted for Michael being held for such a long time. They were going to extract something out of us to not only compensate for the loss of money on Buchanan but also the fact that people were killed." Moore, a dual American and German citizen, was released after 977 days in captivity.

Military rescues are also extremely risky. According to industry data, either a hostage or a rescuer is killed in half of all rescue operations. One tragic example was the 2009 raid carried out by British Special Forces in Afghanistan that freed kidnapped *New York Times* reporter Steve Farrell, but led to the death of a British soldier along with two Afghan civilians, a woman and a child. Farrell's Afghan colleague, journalist Sultan Munadi, was also killed in the raid, and may have been shot accidentally by the British forces. These deaths were all the more tragic because private negotiators who were communicating with the kidnappers already had a deal for both hostages' release. It was not clear that the British government was ever aware.

A dramatic case that tested the resolve of the British authorities came in September of 2011, when a British couple, Judith ("Jude") and David Tebbutt, was attacked by Somali pirates while vacationing in Kenya. Their son Ollie, a twenty-five-year-old furniture designer, was at a job site in Glasgow when a colleague came

78   to tell him that the police wanted to see him. "Because my parents were on holiday, I assumed something bad had happened, like maybe a car crash," Tebbutt recalled. After a weeklong safari, his parents had booked a stay in a secluded resort called the Kiwayu Safari Village on the Kenyan coast. Overnight, Somali kidnappers had raided the property and abducted his mother. His father David was killed trying to resist.

For weeks after being given the news, Ollie was in close contact with the British Foreign and Commonwealth Office, or FCO. He was also visited by representatives from the SO15, the counterterrorism command of the British Metropolitan Police, who were investigating the possible involvement of members of the Al Shabaab militant group in the abduction.

Eventually, Ollie was able to arrange a proof-of-life telephone call with his mother during which he had to break the tragic news that her husband (and his father) had been murdered. The kidnappers wanted huge money—around $10 million.

While his parents had a taste for adventure, they were also careful and meticulous. Ollie discovered that tucked into a travel insurance policy obtained through his father's work was a clause that provided kidnapping and ransom insurance. "It was incredibly lucky, really," Ollie acknowledged.

Through the policy, two security consultants from Control Risks were assigned to the case. "That's when the government said 'you have to make a choice,'" Ollie recalled. "'It's either us or them.'" He found the security consultants to be sober professionals. They explained how the negotiations would work, and that the sole focus would be on getting his mother back alive. "They were very much like, we do this every day, and this

is expected in this part of the world, and this is our pattern for
what a Somali kidnap looks like," he said.

Meanwhile, the government representatives explained
that the British government did not pay ransom, and could not
countenance any arrangement that put money in the hands of
terrorists. This was a problem. While the identity of the kidnappers was murky, the line between Al Shabaab militants,
pirates, and criminals in Somalia was a fluid one. The best
British officials could offer the family was to essentially walk
away—to put what they called "clear water" between the government and any negotiations. Their rather charitable interpretation was that since the kidnappers were demanding
money they had to be criminals.

As an only child, Ollie was the family's point person in the
negotiations. He moved into his parents' home and over the next
six months negotiations were carried out around the kitchen
table. They were surprisingly orderly. Following each phone
call, the kidnappers would make an appointment for a follow
up conversation. Generally, they kept their appointments. A
Control Risks security consultant would brief him on what to
say, and sit by his side. A representative from the Metropolitan
Police monitored the discussions, but did not participate and
did not interfere.

The Tebbutts were a comfortable middle-class family, but
did not have millions of dollars. Ollie found the kidnappers had
a pretty good sense of the value of their hostage, and over the
next few months, under the guidance of the Control Risks negotiator, their demands steadily dropped. They finally agreed to
accept a ransom of around £600,000. The only way Ollie was

80   able to come up with that sum was to use the death benefits he
received following his father's murder.

Ollie and the negotiator traveled to Nairobi for the final
arrangements in March 2012. Control Risks contracted a pilot to
drop the money, but there were some tense moments when the
authorities that controlled the local airstrip outside the town
of Adabo demanded a larger cut. Once that was worked out, and
the kidnappers indicated they were prepared to release their
hostage, things changed. "At that point, the security consultant
drove me to a crossroads in Nairobi," he recalled. "On one side
there was a jeep with the British Foreign Office guys in it and I
just crossed the road and got in their car. That was the last time I
saw anyone from Control Risks."

From that point on, the British government was back in
the game. British officials traveled to the Nairobi airport to collect Jude, and then took her to the British High Commission,
where she was reunited with her son. Jude spent several days
being cared for before she returned home. Eventually, the full
amount of the £600,000 ransom that Ollie had paid was reimbursed under the terms of the K & R policy.

On the one hand, Ollie is grateful that the British government stepped aside and allowed him to pay a ransom despite the
fact that his mother's kidnappers may have been linked to Al
Shabaab. (A British researcher told me that he visited the FCO
office to discuss the case while Jude was being held, and was told
the government was not interested in hearing any information
about the terrorist ties of the kidnappers.) On the other hand,
his experience caused him to focus on what he sees as the hypoc-
risy and heartlessness of the government's position. In order to
apply pressure, Jude's kidnappers were depriving her of food,

slowly starving her to death. If negotiations had dragged on a few more months, "she would have died for sure," Ollie believes.

Ollie is soft-spoken and understated. His voice does not rise, and there is no anger. But he is confused. "The government, their policy is so crazy," he told me. "It makes absolutely no sense. I don't believe for a second that the kidnappers are checking passports or trying to figure out who is from where. They just grab whoever they can. I don't think the British policy protects people in a way that they claim it does, but they are so entrenched in this idea. The idea that they get to choose who a terrorist group is based on pretty flimsy reasons sometimes. Whereas at the same time, governments sell weapons or trade with regimes that are incredibly bad." The logic of the no concessions policy, he believes, is that a certain number of hostages must die in order for the government to show its resolve. If the British government had designated Jude Tebbutt's kidnappers as terrorists, he says, "my Mum would not have come home."

Not everyone who has worked with security consultants has had a positive experience. The most common complaint I heard is that since the consultants are generally made available through the K & R policy the clients have little choice and little recourse if they are assigned someone without local knowledge and experience. Security companies are also businesses. Sometimes they promise more than they deliver. They also charge a lot for their services, so much that average families who don't have insurance generally can't afford them. This also creates resentment.

I interviewed about a dozen hostage negotiators from around the world for this book, and they all told me that they prefer to work closely with law enforcement, so long as the

82   client agrees, which happens in the vast majority of cases. Their first priority is the safety of the hostage, but they also want to see justice done. They also recognize that negotiations can yield intelligence that is useful for ongoing operations and to prevent future crimes. "I do not like the idea of having to give money to criminals," one negotiator acknowledged to me. "That is not something that pleases me at all."

Governments tend to keep security consultants at arm's length. Partly this is a question of creating deniability in sensitive cases, but can also reflect a lack of trust. "The FBI has an institutional culture that emphasizes discretion," a former agent told me. "They are not good at sharing. It makes it frustrating for the families."

Security consultants and private negotiators fill a critical role in hostage recovery, and have an undeniable record of success in criminal cases. They tend to have a lot of experience, and they can provide more intensive support and flexibility for families and businesses undergoing a crisis. They can also front for the family, and do some things that governments can't, such as credibly claim limited resources as a strategy to get the price down. Governments, of course, can't plead poverty. It was only when the Canadian government stepped aside, and the families of Amanda Lindhout and Nigel Brennan brought in a private negotiator, that their case was resolved. Even the French government is beginning to see the advantages, and has instituted a process for licensing private negotiators.

The whole system, as imperfect as it is, breaks down in terrorism-related cases. If the victim is from a no concessions country, security consultants can offer only limited support. If the victim is from a country that negotiates, the private security

consultant is generally asked to step aside while national intelligence agencies takes over. While the security consultants are
pleased to see their clients come home, they are not happy about
the massive payouts.

"The market is now too inflated," said one experienced
security consultant. "Governments have deep pockets and are
basically unable to do what a traditional K&R consultant would
do, which is to put up resistance, to claim an inability to pay, to
bargain, to try and disincentivize the crime."

While such arguments may seem self-serving, they are
borne out in my own research. David Rohde tried to argue with
his captors, who were demanding $25 million and the release
of fifteen prisoners. He told them they were out of touch. They
countered that the French had recently paid $38 million for
the release of an aid worker, and that an Italian journalist had
been ransomed for $15 million and the release of several pris-
oners. Quickly capitulating to high ransom demands—as some
European and Asian governments have done—makes kidnapping more attractive and lucrative around the world. While governments might make a distinction between proscribed and
criminal groups, kidnappers don't. And so the markets are inex-
tricably linked. If a European government pays millions of dollars in ransom to release a hostage held by a terrorist group, then
a criminal group that kidnaps a hapless tourist will expect a
similar payout from a family of modest means that may not have
insurance or the help of a security consultant.

Of course the benefits that security consultants provide—
including to governments—are only available if people have
access to kidnapping and ransom insurance. Governments
should work with the industry to develop innovative ways to

84   extend coverage to vulnerable groups. K & R coverage can be tucked into travel insurance policies—that was why the Trebbutts had coverage—or provided through employers whose staffs operate internationally. For high-risk groups, such as freelance journalists and volunteer aid workers in conflict zones, the challenge is more difficult. But governments can work with the industry to develop specialized products, even if these require public subsidies. Finally, the families of kidnapping victims who lack insurance should be given access to security consultants in extraordinary circumstances, such as in national security cases. This can be done by creating an industrywide pro-bono standard, whereby the security companies increase their volunteer services. It could also be done through some sort of government pool that needy families can access if certain standards are met.

For Doug Milne, who after all is in the business of selling such insurance, a fundamental impediment to extending coverage to high-risk groups is the no concessions framework, which compels insurers to make distinctions between criminal and terrorism cases. In this regard, he believes that the British government's policy is shortsighted. "I strip away the corporate and government stuff and bring it back to the individual," Milne told me. "The right to life is a fundamental human right and if you take away the ability to make concessions you are essentially condemning the person to die. By refusing to allow concessions you drive the negotiations underground so the intelligence you might otherwise get following the case disappears. The families feel they could potentially be prosecuted. And the government becomes the enemy."

The Treasury Official

Inside the White House, Obama administration officials called David S. Cohen their "financial Batman." His job as Undersecretary for Terrorism and Financial Intelligence at the Treasury Department was to cut off terrorist financing, and he oversaw a team of seven hundred and a budget of $200 million. While the position was created during the Bush administration following the September 11 attacks, the role took on a new urgency and prominence under Obama, who was looking for a range of "non-kinetic" strategies to confront the terror threat. Cutting off financing for terror groups would be one way to victory. It was also a lot less costly in terms of human lives. Cohen may have had a bureaucratic title, but he was a four-star general in the financial war on terror.

The myriad terror groups around the world are funded in a variety of ways. FARC made most of its money from the drug trade. Al Qaeda initially received a good deal of its revenue from donations diverted from Islamic charities. It also had wealthy

86   financial backers in the Gulf. The Islamic State, which would not emerge until 2014, relied on extortion, oil sales, and plunder.

At the beginning of the new administration, U.S. officials viewed kidnapping for ransom with increasing concern. "There were a couple of different trends that elevated the importance of the issue," Cohen recalled. "Al Qaeda affiliates were turning to new funding models, including kidnapping. Then there was the spike in piracy off the Somali coast."

While Cohen relied on sanctions and criminal investigations to choke off other forms of terror financing, ransom payments were not coming from rogue actors. Often, they were coming from key U.S. allies in Europe. The best hope for stopping the funding was to forge a global consensus around no concessions. Achieving this objective would require diplomacy and public engagement.

In October 2012, Cohen spoke at Chatham House, the London-based foreign-policy think tank, to lay out the Obama administration's most comprehensive arguments for a global no concessions policy. While Al Qaeda's core operations, centered in Pakistan, had been weakened by the elimination of its top "financial lieutenants," its affiliates, notably in the Sahel and Yemen, were being strengthened financially by the large ransom payments they had been able to collect. AQIM, Cohen noted, citing U.S. intelligence, was targeting Europeans because of their propensity to pay. The money generated had been used to launch large-scale attacks, and to finance expanding operations in Mali that led to the destruction of libraries and Sufi shrines in the cultural center of Timbuktu.

"Simply put, kidnapping for ransom has become today's most significant source of terrorist financing because it has

proven itself a frighteningly successful tactic," Cohen explained.
"Refusing to pay ransoms or to make other concessions to terrorists is, clearly, the surest way to break the cycle because if
kidnappers consistently fail to get what they want they will have
a strong incentive to stop taking hostages in the first place."

Recognizing the obligations of governments to their citizens, of employers to workers, of families to their loved ones,
Cohen acknowledged that, "Not to pay ransom to terrorists is to
jeopardize innocent lives."

"We acknowledge this dilemma—this tragic choice—but
believe that so many lives are at risk of terrorist violence around
the globe that the equation tips decidedly in favor of a 'no concessions' policy," Cohen noted.

Cohen chose to give the speech in London partly because
he wanted to make clear that the U.S. and the UK would have
to work together to forge a global consensus around no concessions. And they would also need to convince the Europeans to
get on board.

Yet, the U.S. policy has historically been inconsistent, even
improvised.

In March 1973, eight members of the Palestinian terrorist group
Black September launched an attack on the Saudi Embassy in
Khartoum, Sudan, and took several diplomats hostage, including
two Americans and one Belgian. They issued a series of demands
that included the release of Palestinian prisoners in Jordan, Israel,
and Europe. They also called for the release of Sirhan Sirhan, who
had been convicted in the 1968 murder of Robert Kennedy.

The following day, President Nixon hosted a scheduled
press conference. A reporter asked how the president planned

88   to respond to the hostage incident. "As far as the United States as a government giving in to blackmail demands, we cannot do so and we will not do so," Nixon proclaimed. "We will do everything we can to get them released but we will not pay blackmail." Within hours, as word of the president's remarks reached Sudan, the three diplomats were taken to a basement in the embassy, stood against a wall, and shot.

Nixon's response at the press conference reflected the political realities of the moment. The president could not even discuss the possibility of releasing the murderer of his likely Democratic opponent in the 1968 presidential elections. But after the hostages were killed no concessions became a "policy sealed in blood," according to Brian Jenkins.

Jenkins, who had served as an Army Green Beret and as a policy analyst in the Defense Department, had joined the RAND Corporation, the Santa Monica-based think tank that often works under contract for the U.S. government. In 1972, he had begun work on a comprehensive study of terrorism, which looked in part at the U.S. response to kidnappings carried out by revolutionary groups in Latin America and around the world. When U.S. diplomats were targeted, the demands were often directed at the national government. In 1969, for example, U.S. Ambassador C. Burke Elbrick was kidnapped by a group of leftist "urban guerrillas" in Brazil. The Nixon administration urged Brazil's military government to do everything necessary to secure Elbrick's release. The Brazilians agreed to release fifteen political prisoners, an action they described as a "humanitarian gesture." Elbrick was freed after four days.

Following the murder of the U.S. diplomats in Sudan, Jenkins expanded his research to look at hostage policies in the handful of countries that took a hard line in domestic kidnapping cases, including Argentina, Guatemala, and Turkey. The UK, which adopted no concessions following the kidnapping of a British diplomat in Uruguay in 1971, was the only global power at the time that embraced the approach. Jenkins and his team found no evidence that refusing to pay ransom led to better outcomes over the short or long term. "We could not come up with a rationale that demonstrated that no-concessions was an effective deterrent," Jenkins recalled.

Jenkins knew that Secretary of State Henry Kissinger opposed negotiations with terrorists. U.S. policy had already been hardening for several years, but the issue remained controversial, particularly among U.S. diplomatic personnel who were asked to undertake high-risk assignments. Some argued the U.S. government should be fully accountable for their welfare, and should take all necessary measures to secure their release in the event they were taken hostage.

As his research progressed, Jenkins held a series of meetings with State Department officials to brief them on the case studies and what he had learned, everything from negotiating tactics to reintegrating returning hostages. When Jenkins briefed Kissinger, he tried to be indirect. "I think I said something like, 'We have been unable to identify convincing empirical evidence to support the presumption upon which the policy is based,'" Jenkins recalled. While Kissinger kept his cool in the meeting, the Secretary of State was not pleased by the findings. He expressed a more "earthy" response with other colleagues.

Jenkins's central finding was that "the most powerful determinant of whether or not there would be further kidnappings is not the policy of the government, but the fate of

90   the kidnappers or their organization. If kidnappers are apprehended and appropriately punished, if kidnapping gangs, or urban guerrilla groups, or terrorist organizations that engage in kidnapping are destroyed, kidnappings will decline. If this is not done, then it doesn't make any difference what the policy is."

The U.S. was already moving toward a more hardline approach to hostage-taking, but the Sudan incident accelerated the shift to no concessions. "Nixon was not thinking about broader policy, he wasn't thinking about all these other issues that ended up being subsequently debated," Jenkins argued. "He was responding to a reporter's question." It was after the fact that "people invented arguments. Of course we couldn't make concessions to terrorist holding hostages because to do so would encourage more kidnappings. Refusing to do so will deter them from doing this again. But all of that came second."

At the time, the no concessions policy was construed quite narrowly to apply only to U.S. government personnel kidnapped or taken hostage overseas. There were no restrictions, nor were any contemplated, on the ability of U.S. families or business people to pay ransom. The FBI often assisted American citizens who chose to do so regardless of whether the kidnapping was carried out by "criminals" or "terrorists."

The no concessions policy also did not apply to hijackings. If a plane were taken hostage, the Federal Aviation Administration would be the lead agency to deal with the incident. Its priority was the safety and welfare of the passengers. In 1972 Nixon himself authorized the payment of a $2 million ransom to three hijackers who took over Southern Airways Flight 49 in Alabama. After a cross-country odyssey, the hijackers, who threatened to crash the plane into a nuclear power plant, landed in Havana, where they were arrested by Cuban authorities. The Cubans returned the plane and the ransom payment.

The no concessions policy also did not apply to U.S. military personnel. U.S. soldiers captured during armed conflict are designated as prisoners of war under the Geneva Conventions, which specifically recognizes the legality of prisoner exchanges.

It did not apply to domestic kidnappings, which, since kidnapping had been made a federal crime in the aftermath of the 1932 Lindbergh baby abduction, had been handled by the FBI. In domestic cases, the FBI had always been willing to negotiate, to facilitate ransom payments from the families, and to sometimes pay directly. In fact, the U.S. Treasury kept up to $300,000 cash on hand at local branches of the Federal Reserve for this explicit purpose. The strategy of paying money was known to FBI negotiators as "ransom as lure," and was considered an effective approach because it often led to the safe release of the hostages as well as the subsequent apprehension of the criminals. "They have to pick up the money somewhere," noted Gary Noesner, who spent thirty years at the FBI, twenty-three of them as a hostage negotiator. "Kidnapping for ransom is a very hard crime to pull off successfully." So much so, that in the last few decades it has all but been eliminated within the borders of the United States and in European countries by effective law enforcement.

And as was made clear years later during the Reagan administration, no concessions was a policy that was often honored in the breach. In a 1985 speech after the hijacking of TWA flight 847 by Hezbollah and Islamic Jihad, President Reagan declared, "America will never make concessions to terrorists—to do so would only invite more terrorism—nor will we ask nor pressure any other government to do so." In fact, the hijacking was resolved after the U.S. pressured Israel to release hundreds of Shia prisoners held in its jails. Later, Reagan authorized arms sales to Iran in violation of the U.S. arms embargo in exchange for Iran's help in resolving the Lebanese hostage crisis, and what began as "arms-for-hostages" later become the Iran-Contra affair. The effort to win the release of the American hostages was largely unsuccessful.

In other words, for nearly three decades following Nixon's proclamation, "we don't negotiate with terrorists" and "we don't make concessions to terrorists" were closer to political slogans than expressions of policy. It wasn't until early in the Bush administration that a decision was made to put a policy on paper. A Hostage Working Group, which met weekly at the White House to review active cases, provided input in formulating a new National Security Policy Directive, to provide policy guidance and ensure coordinated actions across government agencies. The working group, which included the chief of the FBI's Crisis Negotiations Unit, sought to incorporate language that described the tactical reality.

Rather than emphasizing a prohibition on "negotiating with terrorists," the FBI put forward language that described the stated goal as denying hostage-takers "the benefits" of concessions, though it did not rule out ransom if it was part of an effort to both free the hostages and capture the hostage-takers. For the FBI, this was an effort to align the response to international kidnapping with the domestic approach, in which ransom as lure was an important strategy. The working group also proposed adding the word "substantive" to modify "concessions," indicating that while changes in policies, release of prisoners, or ransom payments could not be considered,

minor concessions, like delivering food or making statements
in exchange for the release of hostages, could be on the table.
Both proposals were accepted and incorporated into the final
document.

NSPD-12 covering "United States Citizens Taken Hostage
Abroad" was approved on February 18, 2002. It remains clas-
sified. By the time the new language was finalized, the political landscape had shifted dramatically. The September 11 terror
attacks had occurred, and the beheading of Daniel Pearl had
made it clear that kidnapping was part of the Al Qaeda play-
book. The Patriot Act, passed in October 2001, contained broad
and sweeping language criminalizing material support for terrorism, potentially providing a legal framework to prosecute
families or anyone who assisted or supported the payment of
ransom to designated terrorist groups. Not surprisingly, the
new hostage policy document, which sought to create operational flexibility, sparked a contentious debate at senior levels
of the Bush administration. The most strident objection came
from Defense Secretary Donald Rumsfeld.

The policy debate over the limits of no concessions was theoretical until the following month, when the FBI, taking advantage of operational latitude under NSPD-12, sought to recover
two American hostages held in the Philippines. Martin and
Gracia Burnham, missionaries kidnapped the year before, were
being held in miserable conditions by Abu Sayyaf. The group
had begun as a local insurgency on the southern island of Min-
danao, but had gained international attention through its strategic alliance with Al Qaeda. Seeking to use the ransom-as-lure
strategy, the FBI withdrew $300,000 from the Federal Reserve
in Atlanta and flew it to the Philippines.

94   The ransom was delivered, but unbeknownst to the FBI, Abu Sayyaf had opened up another channel of communications with the Philippine government, and was hoping to collect a second payment. It was a classic double dip. Abu Sayyaf kept the $300,000 but the hostages were not released. There was widespread disappointment and consternation across the National Security Council. The following year, relying on U.S. intelligence, the Philippine government launched a military operation that was more of an assault than a rescue effort. Martin Burnham was shot in the stomach and killed. Gracia was shot in the leg but survived. In 2007, fourteen Abu Sayyaf members were convicted in a Philippine court and sentenced to life in prison for the Burnham kidnapping and the beheading of another American hostage.

After the failed recovery effort in the Burnham case, the ransom-as-lure strategy was never used again during the Bush administration. In Iraq, where FBI negotiators were deployed, kidnap for ransom incidents involving American citizens were dealt with more restrictively on the presumption that terrorist groups were responsible, recalled a former FBI kidnap negotiator. However, very few victims were Americans. The vast majority were Iraqis employed by American contractors, from doctors to truck drivers. In these cases the companies quietly paid ransom. The variable was media attention. Media coverage brought the involvement of senior government officials, which complicated negotiations and limited flexibility. These officials, FBI negotiators grumbled, were far more focused on perceptions and avoiding criticism than resolving the cases.

When Obama took office at the beginning in January 2009, he inherited both NSPD-12 and the Bush administration's conservative interpretation. In May, David Cohen was confirmed as

Assistant Secretary for Terrorist Finance in the Treasury Department. In 2011, he was promoted to Undersecretary. The scope of
his responsibilities was vast, and included implementing sanctions on Russia and Iran. But he was also the lead U.S. official
charged with shutting down the ransom pipeline. Cohen recognized that this could not be achieved without international
cooperation. Countries that pay ransom, Cohen believed, fueled
the overall market for kidnapping and drove up ransom prices,
making the crime more attractive and more lucrative. "You know
what these organizations are going to use the money for," said
Cohen. "To carry out terrorist attacks and kill people."

Based on his own experience, Cohen believed that the
refusal by the U.S. and the UK to pay ransom protected the citizens of both countries. Meanwhile, the competing approaches
in which some countries paid and others did not had a perverse
effect that advanced the hostage-takers' agenda. Kidnappers
could get money from the countries that paid, and victims for
their execution videos from the countries that didn't. The fact
that some countries paid and some didn't also created a framework in which kidnappers sometimes believed that increasing
pressure by abusing hostages or posting terrifying videos would
force countries that claimed not to make concessions to eventually capitulate.

Cohen recognized getting everyone on the same page would
not be easy. One expert I spoke with compared the challenge
to trying to wipe out armed robbery by making it illegal to give
muggers your wallet.

In the effort to build a global standard, France was perceived as
a major challenge. Of course, many countries around the world

96 paid ransom. But the Swiss and the Germans paid quietly. The Italians and Spanish did not have the same global footprint. Qatar and Oman paid, but generally on behalf of other governments. And some Asian countries, like Korea and Japan, had also occasionally paid. But France was different because when a French hostage was taken it often sparked a national mobilization. And when the French president met the returning hostages at the airport, everyone understood why.

Then there was the fact that French president Nicolas Sarkozy was all over the map. He rallied French support for the release of Ingrid Betancourt, a Colombian politician and dual French citizen who had been held captive in Colombia since February 2002. But he adopted more assertive rhetoric and authorized a series of military raids to free French hostages held by Islamic militants.

In the Betancourt case, France used diplomacy and public mobilization to pressure the Colombian government into making concessions that they hoped would lead to Betancourt's eventual release. Beginning in the 1990s, the FARC had turned industrial kidnapping into a steady stream of revenue that it used to fund its military operations. Most of their thousands of victims were Colombians, who were ransomed for money. Betancourt was among the smaller group of about two dozen high profile hostages including three American military contractors who were dubbed "the exchangeables." The goal of the FARC leadership was to trade high-value hostages for their own militants jailed by the Colombian government.

Partly out of indifference and partly because U.S. officials believed that any public statements would only raise their value for the FARC, officials in the Bush administration had been

largely mum about the fate of three American contractors taken
hostage in February, 2003, after their plane crash-landed in
FARC territory while on a drug eradication mission. The three
were being held alongside Betancourt.

This perceived lack of action by the U.S. angered the families of the American hostages, especially after officials blocked
the possible delivery of care packages containing basic neces-
sities like reading glasses and clean clothes. Officials made the
absurd argument that if the goods ended up in the hands of the
FARC it would constitute a violation of the Patriot Act, which
bans material support for terrorist groups.

Meanwhile, the Sarkozy government was deploying diplomatic resources abroad, while supporting public mobilization
at home, which helped keep the Betancourt case in the spotlight. As the head of the support committee for Betancourt,
Florence Aubenas was a constant presence at rallies, public
events, and in the media. These efforts offended the Colombian
government, which believed it was being vilified for its intran-
sigence, while it was the FARC and its cruel tactics that were to
blame for the hostages' fate. "They were telling us to do deals we
weren't willing to do," recalled Colombian Vice President Francisco Santos, referring to the pressure from the French government. "But in turning Ingrid into this important international
figure, it just upped the price for her release."

In fact, at one point early in her captivity, the French government tried to negotiate a ransom for Betancourt. Instead,
the French mediator ended up the victim of a Brazilian scam
artist who claimed to be representing the guerrillas. Later, the
FARC also sought to enlist the French as interlocutors with the
Colombian government for a prisoner exchange deal. Under

98   pressure from Sarkozy, Colombian President Alvaro Uribe
      agreed to release hundreds of FARC prisoners as a goodwill ges-
      ture. The FARC never reciprocated. When rumors surfaced that
      Betancourt was gravely ill, France dispatched a hospital plane in
      the hopes that the FARC would allow their hostage to be treated.

      While the Colombian government resented the pressure, it
      did serve as a reminder that resolving the Betancourt kidnap-
      ping was an international priority. Of course, the Colombian
      government had another motivation, which was that freeing
      Betancourt and the fourteen other high-value hostages would
      deprive FARC of important strategic leverage. Beginning in early
      2008, the Colombian government began to put in place ele-
      ments that would lead to a daring rescue.

      Relying in part on U.S. intelligence, the Colombian military
      was able to identify the approximate location of the hostages'
      jungle hideout. It established a military cordon to contain the
      hostages and prevent them from being moved. On July 2, 2008,
      Colombian agents who had infiltrated the FARC's inner circle
      convinced guards to assemble the hostages in a jungle clearing,
      where a helicopter pretending to be carrying journalists and
      members of the Red Cross would take them to meet with a rebel
      commander. Once the hostages were on board the helicopter,
      their FARC captors were subdued and the hostages freed.

      When word of the rescue reached France, Aubenas declared
      it "Christmas in July." Sarkozy dispatched his Foreign Minister,
      Bernard Kouchner, to Bogotá to escort Betancourt to Paris, where
      the President and First Lady Carla Bruni received Betancourt on
      the tarmac. For a period, she was celebrated as a national hero.

      But Sarkozy took a very different approach with Islamist
      militant groups. Concerned with the mounting toll of French

nationals being taken hostage, particularly in North Africa,   99
Sarkozy promised aggressive action. In July 2010, the president authorized a military rescue of a seventy-eight-year-old
aid worker named Michel Germaneau. The operation killed several AQIM militants, but failed to rescue Germaneau. In retalia-
tion, AQIM beheaded Germaneau, while its leader Abdelmalek
Droukdel declared that "Sarkozy had opened the doors of hell on
himself and his people." Sarkozy responded to the war of words,
calling the raid "a major turning point" in French hostage policy.
But military action did not produce better outcomes, according
to the study by the New America Foundation. Four more hostages were killed in rescue attempts or murdered in reprisal for
failed efforts.

The Sarkozy government also tried to take a harder line
when it came to ransom payments. Part of the recalculation was
a recognition that the groups that were now kidnapping French
nationals were also engaged in action that undermined French
strategic interests, particularly in the case of the AQIM. These
included direct attacks on French regional allies; extortion of
French businesses; and massive smuggling of drugs, cigarettes,
and migrants, who relied on criminal networks for the dangerous
Mediterranean crossing. At one point, Sarkozy tried to imple-
ment a new policy of charging French hostages for government
efforts to secure their release, a move opposed by Kouchner,
who argued it would undermine the security of French journalists and humanitarians working in conflict zones.

As noted in Chapter One, the conflicting desires to secure
the release of French hostages while safeguarding French
strategic interests came to a head with the case of Hervé
Ghesquière and Stéphane Taponier, two journalists kidnapped

100   in Afghanistan in December 2009. The journalists left a French
military embed in Kapisa province to report independently
from surrounding villages. They decided to pursue their story
despite being warned by the French military commander that the
Taliban were active in the area. After the two journalists were kidnapped along with their Afghan assistants, Sarkozy denounced
them as reckless. Aubenas pushed back. "We should not make
these accusations when they are in the hands of terrorists," she
told the president during a meeting.

Aubenas found it particularly galling that at a time when
the journalists were being vilified by French officials she could
not even refer to their records as experienced reporters who
had responsibly covered conflict around the world because
the government had requested a media blackout. On the six
month anniversary of their kidnapping, after the names of the
missing reporters had been released, Aubenas published an
impassioned appeal in *Le Monde* in defense of public advocacy,
writing, "Now that difficult negotiations are underway with the
Taliban group holding the two journalists, many of us believe
that talking about them not only saves them from being forgotten, but protects them. A hostage who matters in the eyes
of public opinion...becomes more valuable and will be better
treated by his captors. A hostage who matters in the eyes of the
public is also like a needle stuck in the daily lives of the leaders
of this country....Remembering each day the existence of these
hostages is, ultimately, defending their integrity, and honoring
a certain ideal of freedom of the press and democracy."

For the next year, until the hostages were finally freed,
the acts of remembrance were constant. There were marches
through the streets of Paris and banners hung in the Luxembourg

Gardens. To mark the two-hundredth day of their captivity, a stage of the Tour de France was dedicated to the missing journalists. When the journalists finally gained their freedom in June 2011, the French government claimed no ransom was paid, while the Afghan government said the journalists were released in exchange for Taliban prisoners. But a detailed account published in *The Daily Beast* and based on reporting from Afghan journalist Sami Yousafzai claimed that neither version was correct. The kidnappers originally presented the French negotiators with a list of fifty Taliban prisoners they wanted released. The French explained that many were held at Bagram Air Base and that they had no leverage with the Americans. Instead, the French offered $10 million in ransom in December, 2010. The deal was rejected by the Taliban, so the French upped the offer to $15 million. The money was eventually delivered to the Taliban in Pakistan.

Cohen visited France and other countries in Europe during this period. He relied on persuasion rather than public shaming to make his case, and was sympathetic to the dilemma that governments faced. In France, he met with a senior French official who was personally supportive of the no concession approach, but also attuned to the political realities of France at that time. "You may be right as a theoretical matter," Cohen recalled the official saying. "But we're not going to abandon our citizens."

Cohen had similar exchanges with other European officials. "I completely understood where they were coming from, why they were taking that view," Cohen recalled. "I think they understood why we were taking the position we were taking, and I never had the sense that anyone disagreed with the basic premise—that this is a good way to dissuade terrorist organizations from taking hostages, and this was an important financial

102   vehicle. I think they probably thought these Americans are cold and heartless, a little bit. My response to that is that it is somewhat cold and heartless as well to allow these terrorist organizations to become very well-funded so they can then go and kill innocent citizens."

Even as France and other Europeans had continued to pay ransom, the U.S. and UK sought to build a global consensus around no concessions. Cohen recognized that ransom payments come from a variety of sources, and he addressed each differently. "I drew a distinction among governments paying, companies paying, and families paying," Cohen explained. "It's hard to expect a family to care about the broader policy implications, and we never made that argument with a family." But he took a tougher line with the insurance industry. "We made clear in various ways that is not a legal defense to a terrorist financing charge that we were paying a terrorist to free a hostage."

Cohen's focus, however, was on forging a consensus among governments, and "we were getting some traction on the issue, and it was encouraging." In December 2009, the UN Security Council adopted Resolution 1904, which condemned Osama bin Laden, the Taliban, and Al Qaeda for its "ongoing and multiple criminal terrorist acts," particularly kidnappings and hostage-takings carried out for the purpose of raising funds or extracting political concessions. The resolution specifically banned the payment of ransom to groups or individuals included on the UN's Consolidated List of Terrorist Organizations and streamlined the process through which groups could be added or removed.

In June 2013, UK Prime Minister David Cameron took another step forward. Chairing the G-8 Summit in Northern

Ireland, Cameron secured a pledge from all its members not to pay ransom and called on international companies to follow suit. "We unequivocally reject the payment of ransoms to terrorists and call on countries and companies around the world to follow our lead and to stamp this out as well as other lucrative sources of income for terrorists," the summit communique read. The consensus was made easier by the bold attack on Algeria's In Amenas gas plant carried out the previous January by the AQIM affiliate led by Mokhtar Belmokhtar. Nearly forty hostages, many of them Europeans, were killed in an assault on the facility conducted by the Algerian military. For Cohen, who worked on the preparations for the summit, the joint declaration was a victory. "Not that it magically transformed the practices of those counties, but it was a pretty high profile embrace of the principal," Cohen noted. "In these endeavors it's step by step."

The next milestone came in January 2014, when the UK followed up on the consensus it had built at the G-8 Summit by putting forward a new UN Security Council resolution that called on states not to pay ransom to terrorists. It was passed unanimously. One provision went further, calling on states to "encourage private sector partners to adopt or follow relevant guidelines for preventing and responding to terrorist kidnappings without paying ransom."

While ransoms were still being paid by European governments under the table, the UN resolution represented a rhetorical recognition of the dangers of such approach. However, the victory was short-lived. Even as the UN resolution was being passed, events were occurring in Syria that would shatter the fragile consensus.

The Aid Workers

In March 2013, Italian aid worker Federico Motka got a new assignment. For the previous year, since relocating from Afghanistan to join Geneva-based Impact Initiatives, Motka had worked all over the world—South Sudan, Peru, and India. Impact Initiatives describes itself as a "think and do tank," and works in partnership with the French humanitarian organization ACTED. Motka's job was to carry out detailed assessments, to visit places confronting humanitarian emergencies, and, based on interviews with local communities, to prepare reports to guide international donors. Motka had recently completed an assessment in southern Syria. Camps of people displaced by the civil war there tended to be settled helter skelter, based on the timing of their arrivals. By organizing the camps along tribal and ethnic lines, aid groups could establish greater social cohesion and improve camp management.

Impressed with his report, the bosses in Geneva now wanted Motka to carry out a similar assessment in northeast Syria. This would be a more a dangerous and difficult task, because Motka would have to navigate active front lines. But the work was vital, and the risk deemed manageable. Motka would also be paired with an experienced "security and logistics coordinator" named David Haines. Haines, a forty-four-year-old former British soldier, had gotten his start during the Bosnian conflict and spent two decades working in war zones around the world.

From his base in Jordan, Motka spent weeks doing preparations and making contacts. Motka recognized that he would be operating in a complex and fluid environment, but neither he nor Haines appreciated the radical transformation that was underway. A new rebel group, incipient and largely invisible outside Syria, was beginning to coalesce. It relied less on international support, and in fact seemed to spend most of its time and energy fighting other rebel groups rather than the government of Bashar al-Assad. The more moderate rebel factions now found it impossible to guarantee the safety of Westerners in their charge. Syrian criminal gangs that had long been involved in kidnapping were also taking advantage of the power vacuum. One key data point that Motka and Haines did not have was that two international journalists, James Foley and John Cantlie, had been kidnapped a few months earlier in the same area where they would be working. For the first several months, their abduction had been "blacked out," meaning it was not reported in the media because it was believed that coverage would complicate efforts to locate and recover the missing pair.

Motka and Haines met up in Turkey, and made their final preparations to enter Syria. The border between Turkey and Syria was only open between noon and 4:30 p.m. each day, so once they crossed over they would have to spend the night. On March 8, they visited displaced communities around Aleppo,

106   then stayed in a house they had rented near the Turkish border. They crossed back into Turkey on Monday, then headed back to Aleppo the following day, Tuesday, March 12. On the way back to their safe house, Motka and Haines made a snap decision to visit the Atmeh refugee camp near the Turkish border. They discussed the risk and the benefits. Motka needed to get a better understanding of the needs of the camp residents relative to families that had returned to their communities near Aleppo. Their security protocol allowed them to respond to circumstances on the ground. But on their way to the camp they passed through a checkpoint that they had not anticipated. Their driver was a bit nervous. It seemed to take a long time for their passports to be returned. "It was weird, but not enough to set off alarm bells," Motka recalled.

After carrying out a quick visit, they were driving back to their guesthouse near the Turkish border when several masked fighters wielding Kalashnikovs approached the car. Motka was on the phone to his boss in Geneva. "I think we are being kidnapped," he said. Then he dropped the phone without switching it off. The kidnappers yanked Motka and Haines from their car, leaving their Syrian driver behind. They threw them in the trunk of their own vehicle, then drove off at high speed. Motka still had his BlackBerry, and struggled in the trunk to type out a message. By the time he hit "send," they were out of range of the Turkish border. The message was never delivered.

After a nearly three-hour-long drive, they were pulled from the trunk. They were in a rural area that Motka suspected was near Idlib. The kidnappers took their passports. "Welcome to Syria," one said in a perfect North London accent. This was one of the Beatles, the name the hostages would give to their sadistic jailers.

Motka and Haines were put in a cell and thoroughly searched. The next day they were taken to the group's leader or "sheik" to be interrogated. It was all very calm and very official, as if, Motka thought, the kidnappers were pretending to be part of the regime. Motka couldn't be sure they weren't. The hostages were blindfolded. Their computers were searched. The interrogators had lots of questions about spreadsheets and maps found on their hard drives. The questions were persistent and aggressive, but not abusive. "Which side do you support?" the sheik asked at one point. Motka tried not to answer, but realized there was no way out. From the trunk of the car, he had heard shouts of Allahu Akbar as he passed through checkpoints. He made the assumption that he was being held by some sort of rebel group. He told his interrogators that, based on what he had witnessed in the camps, he could not support the regime.

Motka had gambled and won. After he declared his opposition to the regime, his treatment improved. But it was now clear he was being held by some sort of Jihadi group, and he and Haines were confronting a long ordeal. Back in their cell, Haines gave Motka advice: Get a routine, always tell the truth, and play the game. Motka said it wasn't until months later that he understood and appreciated the value of these insights. His mission was to play the terrible cards he was dealt and to stay alive.

At his home in Dundee, Scotland, David's brother Mike Haines got a call from ACTED letting him know the terrible news. The British police arrived within minutes. They moved

108   into David's home, setting up security equipment. They carried out detailed interviews. They helped the family rehearse its response should they be contacted by the kidnappers. Within two weeks, the Haines family was invited to London to meet with the Foreign Office. While Mike was told explicitly that the British government would not pay ransom, he was also assured that it would spare no effort to get David back. Prime Minister David Cameron even dropped in on one meeting to ask how the family was coping. The British government picked up the tab for the travel to London, and provided accommodation.

Like his brother David, Mike had served in the British Air Force. They were both aware of the risk associated with humanitarian aid work and the two brothers had spent many hours talking through everything that could go wrong.

"We talked about every scenario and I mean every scenario," Mike explained. "Like if he were abducted by aliens. Like if he were attacked by lions. And we usually had a bottle of brandy. We talked about kidnapping. We talked about ransom. David had always said, 'If you ever pay a pound for my release you will never see me again.'"

"Our family motto is prepare for the worst, hope for the best," Mike continued. "We have a grand tradition of military service. Part of it meant that you don't give in to terrorists. We agree with the government policy. Governments talk to terrorists—it's part of what they do. But you don't pay."

Meanwhile, Motka's family was contacted by the Italian government and brought to Rome for meetings. Italy, alongside Spain, is known for its willingness to pay ransom for the return of its nationals, although it officially denies doing so. In 2004, in a highly publicized case, two Italian aid workers kidnapped in Baghdad were ransomed. The following year, a well-known Italian journalist, Giuliana Sgrena, was also freed in an operation carried out by Italian intelligence. In 2013, the Italian government paid millions for the release of two journalists, an Italian and a Belgian, kidnapped in Syria. While it was never explicitly discussed and no commitments were made, Motka's family hoped that the Italian government would also be willing to pay a ransom to get Motka home.

Back in the Idlib farmhouse, the two hostages recognized that they were on different sides of the no-concessions divide. Haines was philosophically opposed to paying ransom, and had made this abundantly clear to his brother. As a former soldier, he understood and supported his government's policy. But he wanted desperately to live. Motka hoped that a deal could somehow be made for the two of them. They had been kidnapped together, and they should be released together. Meanwhile, their personal situation was deteriorating. After a period of reasonably good treatment, the sheik become convinced that Motka and Haines were acting with defiance and ordered that they be punished. This was a job that the Beatles assumed with relish. The two aid workers were punched, chained, shocked with electricity, waterboarded, and starved. They were told they could not use the bathroom, then beaten when they soiled themselves. Perhaps as a result of the beating, Haines suffered for the rest of his captivity from diarrhea so severe that he could barely eat.

In July, a few days after the start of Ramadan, Motka and Haines were brought together with two other foreign prisoners: journalists James Foley and John Cantlie, who had gone missing the previous November. All four were chained right hand to

110   left hand, and for the first time since their capture they were
moved to a new location. It was a farmhouse, but they called it
the Swedish hotel, because the Jihadi who ran it seemed to be
Scandinavian. All four hostages were in terrible shape, having
been starved and beaten. But in the new environment, they were
allowed to move around freely, to use the bathroom, and given
plenty of food. After five or six days they were moved again, this
time to an abandoned eye hospital in Aleppo.

Not long after they arrived together, Foley, who was raised
Catholic, decided to convert to Islam. "James was quite a religious person," Motka recalled. "For him, it was a way to practice
his religion, to express his religious needs in a way that was safe."

The jailers pressured Motka and Haines to convert as well.
Haines never considered it, but Motka worked through every
scenario. Motka had grown up in the Middle East. His father
worked for Schenker AG, a German logistics and shipping
company, and had relocated the family to the region. Motka
had lived in Baghdad as an infant and been educated in British
schools in the Gulf. He speaks English with a British accent
and often goes by Fred or Freddy. He is highly rational and
deeply analytical, attributes that served him well in carrying
out humanitarian assessments. Now he applied those same
skills to examining his own predicament. He thought that if he
converted, his treatment might improve. But he also believed
there was both a physical and a spiritual risk. If his jailers
believed his conversion was not sincere, he would be punished.
More importantly, he felt that if there was a God—and in that
moment he needed to believe in a higher power—he would one
day have to answer for his deception. He decided he could not
risk his soul.

On June 6, three months after Motka and Haines were kidnapped, French journalist Didier François, and a colleague, Eduard Elias, were detained by rebel forces near Aleppo. François had moved on from *Libération* and was now a reporter for radio station Europe 1. He had covered the Syrian conflict since it emerged in 2011, and had been one of the first to report on the use of chemical weapons by the Assad regime. In a tribute published soon after he was kidnapped, François's friend and colleague, Bernard-Henri Lévy, described his eloquent reports as "written radio."

François and Elias were brought to the eye hospital, whose basement had been converted into a prison for the various rebel forces that sometimes collaborated in the fight against Assad and sometimes competed for control of the city. Fighters from the Al Qaeda-aligned Al-Nusra Front ran one wing, while those from the Islamic State controlled another. The screams of prisoners undergoing torture echoed through the building.

For the first several days of their captivity, François and Elias were handcuffed and chained to a radiator without food or water. Later, they witnessed the beheading of several prisoners through an open cell door. Eventually they were put in a cell with Daniel Rye Ottosen, a former gymnast and aspiring photojournalist from Denmark. Rye had been taken into custody a month earlier in the town of Azaz, during what he planned as a short stint inside Syria to document how civilians were adapting to life during wartime.

The head of the eye hospital prison went by the *nom de guerre* Abu Ubaidah al-Maghribi. He was of Moroccan origin, but a Dutch citizen. Many of the guards were also from Europe, and spoke Danish, Spanish, and French. One, Mehdi Nemmouche, a French citizen of Algerian background, would later carry out an attack on the Jewish Museum in Brussels that left four dead.

In July, only weeks after François and Elias were taken captive, the French Ministry of Defense confirmed that the two were alive and the government was working for their release. The guards informed the hostages that the French government had opened a channel and was negotiating. They also expressed frustration with the Danish government, which had a strict no concessions policy.

On June 22, two other French journalists, Nicolas Hénin and Pierre Torres were detained in Raqqa. They were later brought to Aleppo. American freelance journalist Steven Sotloff was captured in early August. The group shared a room in the eye hospital, but were left alone for extended periods and passed the time telling stories, doing yoga, and playing games fashioned from pieces of cardboard.

Conditions were terrible, but the French hostages were buoyed by the fact that some sort of negotiation seemed to be taking place. The jailers asked for their email contacts and recorded proof of life videos. François, who was the oldest hostage at fifty-three, was elected the "emir." He had had regular contact with the jailers through which he picked up details about the negotiations. François, based on his own experience in the Aubenas case, had a good sense of how things would work. He believed that President Hollande would create a small group of trusted aides to manage the negotiation. He expected that the president would be guided by French national interests, but it did not hurt that he and Hollande were close friends. He

believed that French negotiators would insist the deal would be
for all the French hostages, or none. He knew the government
would be willing to pay, but only if the demand was "reasonable"
and was not a "game changer"—in other words, would not substantially alter conditions on the ground.

What François did not know was that Aubenas—returning
the favor he had once done for her—had agreed to lead the support committee that was rallying for the return of the French
hostages. He did not know that banners were being hung from
buildings in Paris; that rallies were being held in the streets;
and that France's media community had come together to share
information, coordinate coverage, and push the government
toward action.

By late August after the hostages were moved to a new prison
in an industrial area of Aleppo called Sheik Najarr, negotiations
seemed to slow. New hostages joined the group. Marc Marginedas, a journalist from *El Periódico de Catalunya* in Barcelona
arrived with news that was welcomed by Daniel Rye: Denmark
had won the Eurovision song contest. Two other Spanish journalists, Javier Espinosa from the national daily *El Mundo* and photographer Ricardo García Vilanova, had been detained in Raqqa
in mid-September. They were later brought to Aleppo along
with U.S. aid worker Peter Kassig. They were journalists and aid
workers, for the most part, and came from a variety of countries,
including the U.S., the UK, France, Spain, Italy, Belgium, and Germany. None of them knew exactly why they had been taken.

For the hostages themselves, the bad news was that
the Beatles were back in the picture. They showed up in
November 2013, and adopted a much harsher tone than the
French-speaking guards who had looked after the hostages in

114   the eye hospital. The Spanish journalists theorized that the
Beatles sought to create their own version of Guantanamo, filled
with prisoners dressed in the same clothes and experiencing
the same abuse and humiliation as Muslim prisoners held at
the U.S. military base. Guantanamo was something the guards
talked about constantly. "George," one the Beatles, came up with
the idea of making all the prisoners wear orange jumpsuits, and
proudly showed off the fabric when it was delivered.

For Motka, the parallels with Guantanamo were less a
well-considered propaganda strategy than a reflection of the
eye-for-an-eye mentality that guided the guards' every action.
He recalled that when he, David, John, and Jim were being held
in Idlib, before the move to Aleppo, the guards made them all
read a news story about Aafia Siddiqui, the MIT-educated
Pakistani neuroscientist and alleged Al Qaeda operative, who
had been imprisoned in the U.S. The article claimed that Siddiqui was beaten in the Texas prison where she is serving an
eighty-six-year sentence for attempted murder. As soon as the
hostages finished reading the article the guards set on them and
beat them mercilessly. This was also the period when all four
hostages were waterboarded.

Motka had a different theory. He believed—or at least he
hoped—that the hostages had been brought together because
the kidnappers intended to ransom them as group. Indeed,
by the fall of 2013 there seemed to be new and more systematic effort to negotiate, this time led by the Beatles. All the hostages were asked to provide email address for their families and
employers and a flurry of messages was sent out in November
and December 2013. The message sent to Motka's family read,
"Our demands for this negotiation are: Primarily, that you

influence your government however you can to release our
Muslim prisoners in exchange for Fedrico. However if this is
unsuccessful due to your lack of influence or your government
simply not caring then the amount of 100,000,000 euro's will
be accepted as our secondary demand." This was substantially
similar to the email sent other families, including the Sotloffs
and Foleys.

Despite the misspellings and typos, Motka said the message was carefully crafted to ensure that the demands were reli-
giously justified, at least in the minds of his jailers. The Prophet
Mohammed, the Beatles explained, had sought to exchange
prisoners with his enemies, and had only accepted money when
this was not possible.

This new round of negotiations forced each of the hostages
to consider his particular fate. At one point, Foley, aware of the
U.S. no concessions policy, proposed to François that the French
lead negotiations on behalf of all the hostages. He even suggested
that Qatar could be convinced to pay the ransom. But François
told him that he knew how the French operated and said he could
not risk his own life or that of his French colleagues on a new and
untested approach. François believed that a channel had been
opened, and that the French government would reach out to the
other governments who could choose to negotiate or not, based
on their own principles or interests. However, my own reporting
efforts suggest this may not have been the case. Sources in the
U.S. and Spain told me they were never contacted by the French,
and that they did not share information about the negotiations.

In mid-September 2013, soon after Javier Espinosa and Ricardo
García Vilanova were detained in Raqqa, Pedro J. Ramírez, the

editor of *El Mundo*, got a call from Javier's wife, Mónica Prieto. Mónica and Javier were a formidable reporting duo and had covered some of the region's worst violence. The year before, Espinosa had survived the shelling of the press center in Homs that killed two of his colleagues, including the *Sunday Times* correspondent Marie Colvin. The couple now lived in Beirut with their two young children.

"It was a very emotional moment," Ramírez recalled. "In the newsroom of *El Mundo*, we had various colleagues killed over the years." In May 2000, columnist José Luis López de Lacalle was assassinated by an ETA hit squad outside his home in Spain's Basque Country. In 2003, reporter Julio Anguita Parrado was killed in a missile attack while embedded with U.S. forces in Iraq. In 2001, Julio Fuentes was gunned down in Afghanistan along with a group of international reporters. An Afghan man later convicted of the crime claimed he was ordered by a top Taliban commander to execute the journalists. Prieto was married to Fuentes and she and Ramírez traveled to Pakistan to collect his body. Ramírez was determined to do all he could to ensure that Prieto was not widowed a second time.

Ramírez is a legendary figure in Spanish journalism. At twenty-eight, he became the youngest editor of a national daily when he took over the struggling *Diario 16*. After turning it around, he left in 1989 to found a new daily, *El Mundo,* which, though linked to the right-wing Popular Party, was quite liberal on social issues. The paper was also known for its investigations and its uncompromising stance against Basque separatists. In 1989, officials in Spain's Socialist government leaked a sex tape in a failed attempt to extort Ramírez and get *El Mundo* to change its editorial positions. Along with his wife, designer Agatha Ruiz

de la Prada (from whom he separated in 2017), Ramírez was half
of Madrid's ultimate power couple. Now, with the life of two
reporters in the balance he got on the phone with General Sanz
Roldán. The two would stay in touch throughout the crisis.

The challenge for the CNI was that Spain did not have a great
network of contacts in the Middle East. In a notorious 2003
incident, seven Spanish CNI agents were killed in an ambush
in Iraq, leaving a gaping hole in their intelligence network. Fortunately, Prieto had her own contacts built up over many years
of reporting in the region. The CNI assigned an agent based in
Beirut to work with Prieto on the recovery effort.

When Espinosa and Prieto had worked in Iraq, they developed a protocol to deal with the risk of kidnapping. They moved
in convoys, with a motorcycle deployed ahead to pass through
the checkpoints and radio back if there were problems. Espinosa
grew out his beard, and they both dressed in local clothing. They
tried to speak as little as possible in public. But in Syria, conditions were changing rapidly, and they were not aware journalists were being targeted. "We didn't connect the dots," Espinosa
admitted later.

Still, Prieto become aware within hours that something was
wrong, after Espinosa missed his regular check-in. She knew
that he and García Vilanova were on the road from Raqqa to the
Turkish border. Had there been fighting? Had they been detained?

Over the next few weeks, working her sources and contacts
in Syria, Prieto was able to confirm that her husband and his
colleague had been detained at a checkpoint and were being held
in Raqqa. She met with every influential Jihadi she could think
of to plead her case, even traveling to Istanbul to lobby leaders of
various rebel groups who had gathered for a meeting with their

118   Gulf financiers. At first, Prieto simply fed what she had to the
       CNI agent she was working with. But he was a quick learner, and
       by the end of the summer had developed his own sources. They
       were able to locate the specific house where the hostages were
       being held. Fearful that the U.S. military would try to launch a
       rescue attempt, they made a decision not to share the informa-
       tion with the U.S. government. Prieto was never contacted by
       the FBI or any U.S. authorities.

       In December, after a three-month blackout in which the
       kidnapping of the Spanish journalists was not reported, Prieto
       decided to hold a press conference in Beirut. "Javier didn't only
       survive the bombardment of Baba Amr, which killed two of his
       colleagues right before his eyes," Prieto declared. "He even chose
       to stay in the neighborhood until the last civilian was evacu-
       ated....When I asked him to leave before the fall of Homs, he told
       me he had the obligation to stay and report. I reminded him that
       our children needed him alive, and he replied by telling me that
       the children of Syria needed the world's attention."

       It was not until near the end of the year, when the emails
       went out to all the hostage families, that Prieto finally made
       contact with the kidnappers. Some messages were encouraging,
       others terrifying and insulting. When the negotiations reached
       a point where particulars were being discussed, Prieto told the
       kidnappers that she was concerned about the security of her
       email and so had created a new account. In fact, that account
       went directly to the CNI agent, who handled the negotiations
       from that point forward. Prieto was kept out of the loop.

       Meanwhile, back in Madrid, Pedro J. Ramírez was forced
       out as editor of *El Mundo*. The paper said it was a finan-
       cial decision, but Ramírez alleged payback for reporting on

corruption in the administration of President Mariano Rajoy.
Despite his ouster, Ramírez made the decision to stay on at *El Mundo* in a non-executive role in part to support Prieto. Casimiro García-Abadillo, Ramírez's deputy who took over as editor-in-chief, told me the final round of ransom negotiations were handled through a contact in Qatar "connected to the kingdom's security or intelligence." He said that the demands were strictly economic and not political but that he did not know the final amount paid. Ramírez believes the money was paid by the CNI from its "reserve funds," but never received confirmation. When I spoke with *El Mundo*'s owner, Antonio Fernandez-Galiano, he said he knew nothing about the details, which were handled entirely by the CNI.

During the many years in which the Basque separatist group ETA was active in Spain, *El Mundo* had taken a hard line against the payment of ransom in domestic kidnappings. But Ramírez saw no contradictions in paying ransom to secure the release of Spanish journalists abroad. "I've always maintained that each circumstance has to be judged on its own merit," Ramírez argued. "Even if you have a general principle of not paying ransom, there are always exceptional circumstances. Even with ETA, the government adopted a firm posture of not negotiating, but through underground channels helped facilitate the negotiations for families that wanted to pay."

"You have to consider which option is the least bad," Ramírez continued. "Probably we are confronting what Isaiah Berlin called the conflict of negative liberty in which any decision taken has negative consequences. But I believe that the authorities in a democratic country should be especially concerned when a journalist is kidnapped or detained by a military

120   while exercising his profession. It seems correct and logical that the secret services worked to secure Javier's release."

Ramírez acknowledged that the calculus might be different for the United States because of its military involvement in the region. "Spain has peacekeeping forces in some places, but it's a symbolic and marginal presence. I understand that the U.S. authorities see their hostages as an instrument of coercion in the face of a foreign or defense policy. This is something that has been taken into account. But in the case of a country like Spain, this is a very secondary question."

"It's looking good for the Spaniards," George, the leader of the Beatles, announced in February 2014. A few weeks later, the Beatles entered the room in a house outside Raqqa that the hostages called the Quarry. The hostages had been moved to Raqqa in January, 2014 after a combined rebel offensive in Aleppo drove the Islamic State from the city. Now, George announced, everyone needed to pack their belongings. Marc Marginedas was being released and the rest of the hostages were being moved. It was not a surprise that Marginedas was the first to be freed, since the other hostages knew he was suffering from a medical condition that required treatment. The hostages were loaded into cars, according to Motka's recollection, and driven around in circles and then returned directly to the same house. Marginedas was no longer among them. The purpose of the ruse was to ensure that Marginedas believed the hostages were no longer in the same location, and would inform the intelligence agencies accordingly.

In early March, the Beatles removed a Russian hostage, Sergey Gorbunov, and shot him in the head. They forced the remaining captives to view pictures of Gorbunov's execution that they shared on a laptop. They promised that all would suffer the same fate if a ransom was not forthcoming. On March 30, Espinosa and García Vilanova were released. This time the Beatles announced that the hostages were being moved, but didn't even bother to drive them around.

In April, when the four French hostages were released, the Beatles simply walked in and ordered them to pack up their things. Just before they were freed, the Beatles brought in Kayla Mueller, an American aid worker who had been captured in August 2013, but had been kept apart from the men. Mueller asked the French hostages to inform the U.S. authorities that they would be freed in exchange for release of Aafia Siddiqui and 5 million euros in cash. This same demand would be conveyed to Mueller's family via email the next month. As he was departing, George also whispered into François's ear terms for the release of the other Americans, Foley, Sotloff, and Kassig.

The French hostages returned home to a hero's welcome. President Hollande declared that France was proud to have secured their release. François responded that the hostages were lucky to be French. After some hesitation, François agreed to speak with the FBI's legal attache at the U.S. Embassy in Paris. He provided information on the location of the house where the hostages were held, and the terms for the release of the American hostages. He has never publicly discussed the details of the offer. When I talked with well-placed U.S. officials, they told me they had never seen anything specific conveyed via François.

François had also carried a letter from David Haines. This was the only contact that his brother Mike had with him through the entire kidnapping ordeal. The letter used an agreed-upon

122   code to indicate that it had been written under duress. The only
genuine sentiment it contained was a desire from David to send
all his love to his daughters. This Mike duly did.

Next to be released were three women who worked for
Medecins San Frontieres, followed by two men, nationals of
Denmark and Belgium. Their negotiations were handled by MSF
directly on a separate track from the other hostages. Dan, whose
last name has not been made public, smuggled out a letter from
Kayla Mueller to her parents in his enormous beard. Mueller and
the male hostages had been exchanging messages left in their
shared bathroom, a breach of the rules that the Beatles eventually discovered.

Motka was released at the end of May. The Italian government has never discussed with Motka or his family how the
hostage negotiations were handled. In January, 2014 the Italian
government paid an estimated $11 million for two aid workers
kidnapped in Syria. Photos of the cash piled high on a desk were
featured in an Al Jazeera documentary. Motka assumes a similar intelligence operation delivered the ransom that led to his
freedom.

The last two hostages to be released were Daniel Rye and
a German aid worker named Toni Neukirch. Since Denmark
does not pay ransom, Rye's family had to raise 2 million euros
on their own. They could not have done so without the help of
a security consultant, whose fees were partially covered by a K
& R insurance policy that Rye had acquired before his trip to
Syria. The man, who I spoke with but who asked not to be identified, delivered a black knapsack stuffed with cash to two men
on a motorcycle who met him at a designated drop point on the
Turkish-Syrian border. The same consultant was also part of a

team that worked on the Foley case. Their fees were covered   123
by a K & R policy acquired through the *Global Post*, Foley's media
outlet. They were the only two of the ISIS hostages known to
have had active policies.

Motka believed until the end that the kidnappers were interested in negotiating for the release of other hostages, including
his colleague David Haines, but there was plenty of evidence this
was not the case. The American and British hostages were not
asked to provide proof of life, even as the negotiations proceeded
for the release of the other hostages. When the Spanish hostage
Marc Marginedas was released, the jailers ordered James Foley
to take a good look, announcing "this is a close as you will get
to freedom." They beat Foley repeatedly, accusing him, falsely,
of having served in the U.S. military. At one point, the kidnappers forced the remaining hostages to witness an execution
while holding signs demanding that their ransom be paid. But
the Americans and Brits were left behind. Six new orange jumpsuits were delivered so that the British and American hostages
could record videos making impossible demands, like a ransom
of $100 million and the release of Muslim prisoners held by the
U.S. Recognizing his likely fate, Foley dictated a letter to his
family that Rye memorized and read to them once he was freed.
While the Beatles encouraged Rye's family to raise the ransom
money and set an exorbitant though obtainable demand, there
was no comparable effort for the American or British hostages.

On July 3, 2014, about a month after the last European hostage was freed, the U.S. military launched a raid and rescue
operation codenamed Graphite Arrow. Based on intelligence
gathered from the freed hostages, operators from Delta Force
backed by helicopter gunships and armed drones targeted

124 the building that the hostages had called the Quarry. It had taken time for the U.S. to organize the raid because it had to cross-check intelligence and locate the building using satellite imagery, according to an account published in the *New Yorker*. Motka found this odd, because after the first hostages were released in early March, the remaining hostages were held in the same building until at least early June, when Daniel Rye and Toni Neukirch were released. While in captivity, Motka had climbed on the shoulders of Dan from MSF to peer out a vent in their cell. Based on what he saw, Motka draw a map on a napkin while riding on the plane back to Italy. Later, he was able to locate the building where he was held on a Google map. He alerted Italian intelligence, and later debriefed the FBI and the British Metropolitan police. In any case, the remaining hostages had been moved by the time the American raid took place. The mission came up empty, except for communications equipment and other intelligence recovered from the house. Two ISIS fighters were killed in the raid, and a U.S. helicopter pilot was seriously injured.

The military raid had been authorized by President Obama because he believed the fate of the remaining hostages had effectively been sealed. The bombing campaign by U.S. forces that began in August 2014 in response to the massacre of Yazidi civilians on Mount Sinjar and the ISIS takeover of the Iraqi city of Mosul provided the political cover that ISIS needed to carry out their ghastly executions.

The value of the terrorizing propaganda is suggested by the fact that Foley's execution was filmed by several cameras and meticulously edited. According to an analysis carried out by Javier Lesaca, a Spanish academic, ISIS videos tended to focus on four areas, effective administration of their quasi-state, testimonials from young people drawn to the cause, their prowess in battle, and the execution of prisoners. The videos were modeled on popular video games and violent movies like *SAW*, *Call of Duty*, *American Sniper*, and *The Hunger Games*. While Al-Qaeda videos showed a "bunch of old guys in a cave," ISIS videos were dynamic and featured the voices of the young multicultural recruits, not their middle-aged leaders. A key function of the videos was recruitment. ISIS recruiters would track engagement with the content, and reach out via direct message on Twitter to anyone who reacted positively. In this sense, the execution videos were worth far more to ISIS than any ransom payment they might have received.

The Foley execution video was uploaded on August 19. Two weeks later, Steven Sotloff was murdered, followed by David Haines. Alan Henning, a British taxi driver, was murdered in October. Peter Kassig was killed the following month.

Even as ISIS was murdering the male hostages, they continued to negotiate for the release of Kayla Mueller. Following up on the email sent in May 2014 demanding 5 million euros and the release of Aafia Siddiqui, they sent a note in June demonstrating a sophisticated understanding of how hostage negotiations work. Insisting that organizations that work in conflict zones have "special insurance" and that "governments DO pay ransoms! (when it's done under the table)" the kidnappers reiterated their financial demands. But they also added a new argument. The release of five high-value prisoners from Guantanamo in exchange for U.S. soldier Bowe Bergdahl made their "one-for-one" demand of Mueller for Siddiqui eminently reasonable. The next note, sent July 12, adopted an angrier and

126   more strident tone. It referenced the "miserably failed" rescue
       attempt and said Kayla would be killed in thirty days if the
       family failed to come up with the money. By September, a
       new condition had been added: The U.S. must stop its "crim-
       inal aerial bombardments of the Islamic State." In February
       2015, ISIS claimed that Mueller had been killed in a Jordanian
       air strike, and sent the family a photo of her battered body. Her
       family believes Mueller may have been murdered by her cap-
       tors, although this has never been confirmed. Two Yazidi girls
       who escaped from sexual slavery claimed that Mueller had been
       held prisoner in the home of a top ISIS commander known as
       Abu Sayyaf, and repeatedly raped by the group's leader Abu Bakr
       al-Baghdadi. A May 2015 raid carried out by the U.S. military
       killed Abu Sayyaf and captured his wife. Under interrogation,
       she confirmed the abuse.

       For the American families, the death of the American
       hostages demonstrated the fecklessness of the U.S. hostage
       policy. Unlike the British hostage families, all of the Americans
       claimed a lack of support, cooperation, and even basic empathy
       on the part of U.S. officials. The families were told to keep quiet
       and avoid the media. Initially, they had no contact with each
       other, a function of U.S. State Department regulations which
       prohibits the sharing of "private information." At a notorious
       White House Department meeting in May 2014, Mark Mitchell,
       the NSC Director of Counterterrorism and a retired Army col-
       onel, informed the families that paying ransom was illegal and
       families could be prosecuted. "We were told face to face, we
       don't negotiate with terrorists," Art Sotloff, the father of Steven
       Sotloff, told me. "It is against the law; you could be prosecuted;
       anyone that aids or abets could be prosecuted." Mitchell later

defended his actions, saying he wanted families to be made
aware of the legal risk, and to understand that while hostage
recovery is a priority it is not necessarily the top priority.

A source at the U.S. State Department who worked on the
hostage cases told me that despite Mitchell's warning the families were repeatedly reassured that they would not be prosecuted for paying ransom. They were also told that the no
concessions policy was intended to give the families leverage in
the negotiations with their kidnappers, allowing them to argue
that they were on their own and could not afford the huge sums
being demanded. But as someone who was in touch with several of the families during this period, I can affirm that they—as
well as those who were trying to help them—were uncertain of
their legal position. The notion that the no concessions policy
would give families leverage was belied by the experience of the
Muellers, who received nothing but scorn when they told Kayla's kidnappers they were seeking to raise money on their own
without the help of the U.S. government. In fact, the executions of American and British hostages so dramatically changed
the calculus for the U.S. government that at one point State
Department officers broached the idea of the American government finding a way to pay the $5 million the Islamic State
was demanding for Mueller's release. The idea was quickly shot
down by more senior officials who made it clear this would represent a violation of U.S. policy.

The ambiguity around the U.S. position also stifled private
efforts to win the release of the hostages, according to David
Bradley. Bradley, the owner of *The Atlantic*, was moved by the
experience of his own reporter, a freelancer abducted in Libya
in 2011, to launch a personal campaign in support of the hostage

128   families. In his travels around the world to investigate the cases
        of the missing Americans, "we just never came across the U.S.
        government," Bradley told me. "I would ask people, 'Are you
        talking to the U.S. government?' Maybe out of 150 we met, three
        times we crossed paths with the government investigation."

        "I found the U.S. government in the early days not just
        unhelpful but an impediment to doing the work," Bradley con-
        tinued. "The Obama administration's strong view, coming
        from the president himself, but down to the National Security
        Council, and out to the agencies, was that the United States does
        not pay ransom. And I know it's a very well-intended policy, but
        it also had a chilling effect, it meant that allies around the world
        were concerned not to help the U.S. government for fear of being
        seen as paying ransom."

        On several occasions, beginning at the end of 2013, Bradley
        and former FBI agent Ali Soufan traveled to Qatar, where they
        met with Ghanem Khalifa al-Kubaisi, the head of the kingdom's
        Intelligence Service, to ask for help in securing the release of
        Foley and Theo Padnos, an American freelance journalist kid-
        napped by the Al Qaeda affiliated Al-Nusra Front. Bradley
        delivered the talking points provided by the FBI and the State
        Department, declaring "the United States does not pay ransom,
        and I as a private citizen, am not allowed to pay ransoms and I
        don't want you to pay ransom but can you help us in any way?"
        The Qataris promised to be helpful. Padnos was released on
        August 24 after two years in captivity and only days after Foley
        was murdered. The Qataris said no ransom was paid, and that
        Padnos was released on a humanitarian basis. Given Qatar's
        record of paying ransom in other cases, many experts I spoke
        with were highly skeptical of the claim. In a 2018 interview with

the Saudi-owned broadcaster *Al Arabiya*, Padnos himself said
he suspected that Qatar paid a ransom for his release as part of a
strategy to channel money to the Al-Nusra Front without running afoul of its Western allies.

Motka does not believe the Beatles had started out with
some master plan to exploit the differences in hostage policies. Like the hostages themselves, they had simply "played the
game" and stumbled into an opportunity. When they made
the decision to kill the American and British hostages rather
than ransoming them is difficult to discern, and many of those
I spoke with, including intelligence officials, security consultants, and the hostages themselves, have different views. My
own conclusion, based on interviews with the surviving hostages who described the shifting treatment of the Americans and Brits, is that ISIS initially intended to ransom all the
hostages, either together or separately. At some point in early
2014, that changed. While the murders were not a specific reac-
tion to the American bombing campaign or to the failed rescue
attempt, those events may have reinforced the determination to
carry through on their brutal plan.

The ransoming of European hostages and the videotaped
murders of the American and British hostages was a huge propaganda victory from ISIS's perspective, allowing them to highlight their political demands while making the U.S. in particular
appear indifferent to the plight of its own citizens. Each hostage
I spoke with viewed the issue through their own perspective.
Javier Espinosa told me that "foreign policy rather than hostage
policy" determined who lived and who died.

At the time that David Haines was kidnapped, both and he
and Mike were firm supporters of the British no concessions

130   policy. But as David watched the European hostages being ransomed one by one, his commitment began to waver, according to Motka. More than anything else, David wanted to see his two girls again. "You can say you are opposed to paying ransom, but until you are in that situation you don't know how you are going to react," Mike pointed out when we spoke. Mike told me that he watched the Europeans being freed and thought, "those bastards—they gave in."

The anguish that Mike feels is reflected in the convoluted thinking required to make sense of his brother's death. "My family knows where I stand—no ransoms," he said. "I think the British and American policy is the right one. David always said that if you pay ransom, it will just be used to buy weapons for terrorists. Still, if I had it within my power, I would have paid a ransom to get David back. Even if my brother never spoke with me again."

Mike is also grateful that Motka was ransomed. "I am so glad that Fred got out," he said. "Fred is as close to me as David. I know that Fred has such an immense amount of guilt. As do the other hostages."

By March 2015, Motka, who had settled in London after winning his freedom, attended a lecture by Jonathan Powell at the London School of Economics. Powell, the former chief of staff to Tony Blair, had written an acclaimed book entitled *Talking to Terrorists: How to End Armed Conflict*. Drawing on his experience as chief British negotiator on Northern Ireland, Powell argued that while governments claim they will not talk to terrorists, in the end nearly all do. They do so out of strategic interests—because dialogue is the only way to end a conflict. Recognizing this inevitable dynamic, governments can

save lives by engaging with so-called terrorists at the outset.
Even engagement with Al Qaeda and the Islamic State, Powell
argued, must be considered.

Not surprisingly given the recent murders of Haines and
other British hostages in Syria, one of the first questions out
of the audience was about the British no concessions policy. "I
don't work on hostages because it's a different sort of discipline
from political negotiations," Powell conceded. "The question of
whether you should negotiate over hostages is a classic prisoner's dilemma. If you're an individual hostage, you'd very much
like them to negotiate on your behalf. But the reason that the
British and the Americans and others have been trying to per-
suade the French and the Italians and other governments not to
pay ransom is because it encourages further kidnappings and
funds terrorist groups to a large extent."

Motka, still reeling from having left Haines behind, left the
event feeling angry and disappointed. He had similar debates
with Haines during their shared captivity, so the answers were
not merely academic. "To me it sounded completely schizo-
phrenic, in the sense that you are saying you can talk to the
Islamic State but you can't talk about hostages," Motka told me.
"This can't be a black and white discussion. We are living in a
gray world. Your principles are not your policy."

The Parents

During the eighteen months that Jim Foley was held hostage in Syria, his parents, John and Diane, sought to make their son's return a priority for the U.S. government. They were able to secure a meeting in the White House with National Security Advisor Susan Rice, whom Diane had gotten to know when Rice served as U.S. Ambassador to the United Nations. While Rice was sympathetic, she referred Diane back to the FBI. Diane was disappointed. She believed that it was only President Obama himself who could cut through the bureaucratic infighting and "make things happen."

On the day that Foley's execution was uploaded to YouTube on August 19, 2014, Obama was en route to Martha's Vineyard for a family vacation. Lisa Monaco, the president's Homeland Security and Counterterrorism Advisor, watched the video and was in tears when she called NSC's deputy security advisor Ben Rhodes on board Air Force One and asked him to inform the president. "Foley the journalist?" Obama responded upon

hearing the news. "I should call the family. And make some kind
of statement."

Rhodes, also one of Obama's chief speechwriters, drafted the statement that night in the vacation home where the president and his family were staying while the Obamas were having dinner with friends in the dining room. By the end of the evening, the president's position had hardened and he argued that they should just release the statement rather than making a public appearance. But Rhodes and White House Chief of Staff Denis McDonough urged Obama to speak to the media the next morning.

"People need to hear from you on this one, Mr. President," McDonough argued.

"OK," the president said. "But I think it just elevates ISIL." (ISIL is what the administration called the Islamic State.)

The next morning, after calling the Foleys to offer his condolences, Obama spoke to the press. He praised Foley as a man "who lived his work." He heaped scorn on the Islamic State. "No just god would stand for what they did yesterday and for what they do every single day," he declared. Privately, he complained that his remarks gave the terrorists "exactly what they want." After finishing his statement, Obama headed to the golf course where he was photographed laughing with friends. Facing withering criticism, he acknowledged that his golf outing had produced bad "optics."

In January 2013, the Foleys had made a decision to go public about their son's kidnapping. Public appeals can put pressure on governments, but they also have the potential to drive up demands and complicate negotiations. Other hostage families,

134   including the family of John Cantlie, who was kidnapped along-side Foley, had decided to keep quiet.

While the Foleys were not able to use the profile they gained through their public campaign to bring their son home, after his death they discovered they had an important platform. They decided to use it to highlight the U.S. government's dysfunction and to push for change.

In media interviews and public appearances, the Foleys talked openly and with unusual bluntness about the failure of the U.S. government to coordinate its response. They described the way they were shunted from agency to agency, and spoke with outrage about the heartless lecture they received from Mark Mitchell in May 2014, when he warned the Foleys and other families that they could be prosecuted for paying ransom. Mitchell also told the families that the U.S. would not conduct a military raid to rescue the hostages and would not ask another country to intervene on their behalf.

Three months after Jim's murder, in November 2014, Diane was finally able to meet with President Obama at the White House. "Jim was always our top priority," Obama told her.

"With all due respect, Mr. President," Diane responded, breaking into tears. "You know he never was."

The president didn't argue. He told Diane that the U.S. had failed them and other American families.

Before Jim's disappearance, Diane Foley was a nurse prac-titioner in a small town in New Hampshire. John is a doctor. Diane had never done media, never been an advocate, never been a spokesperson for a cause. But she discovered she had all the qualities she needed to succeed in her accidental role. She is an effective networker; a keen observer of facts; an efficient

researcher; and an articulate public speaker. She is confident in
her conclusions; polite and considerate in her personal dealings,
but willing to ask uncomfortable questions and call things as
she sees them. "Our original FBI guy was a joke," Diane insisted
when I asked her about her first interactions with the U.S. government. "He spoke no Arabic. He just sits here and suggests
to us that we talk to President Assad, who could help us. It was
laughable."

Diane's candor got attention, but it also rankled some
people in the U.S. government who had worked on Jim's case. Of
course not all hostage families are as outspoken, or as aggrieved.
But the Foleys' media visibility gave them the floor and the
ability to shape perceptions.

During the period that Jim was in captivity, Diane made two
unaccompanied trips to Europe after the Spanish and French
hostages were released. She was impressed with the French
way of doing things. She met with Didier Le Bret, the head of
the French government Crisis Cell. Le Bret was shocked about
how little Diane had been told and aghast the U.S. did not have
a person—or a system—responsible for keeping her informed.
"I was absolutely puzzled," Le Bret told me. "She knew nothing.
All the work was happening behind locked doors. There was no
single point of contact. No human relationship. The emphasis
of U.S. no concession was displaying no signs of weakness—but
the needs of the family had been forgotten in the process."

Diane and John also met with Florence Aubenas and the
support committee, who were working for the release of Didier
François and the other French hostages held in Syria. They
attended a bimonthly meeting of the "media group" where representatives from different media organizations got together to

136   compare reports, vet rumors, and coordinate responses. "That's the way French journalists really got the public behind them, to push the government," Diane recalled. "There's this advocacy feeling in France. They love their journalists."

The Foleys wanted to apply some of the French experience in the U.S. They wanted greater media solidarity, with U.S. journalists not just covering events but working behind the scenes to put pressure on officials. They wanted greater coordination within the government agencies. They wanted greater compassion and sympathy. And while they didn't challenge the U.S. no concessions policy, they noted repeatedly that the European governments that paid ransom got their hostages home, while the American and British hostages were killed.

"I want to continue Jim's work," Diane told a packed house at the Newseum in Washington in February 2015. "He would want to right this wrong. Our government can do better. Our press can do better. I hope part of Jim's legacy can be to stimulate this discussion and to advocate for a clearer policy that will bring our citizens home." Doug Frantz, a former *New York Times* and *Los Angeles Times* reporter who had become Assistant Secretary of State for Public Affairs, represented the government's perspective on the panel. Frantz spoke about how the U.S. government had failed to anticipate the brutality of the Islamic State's tactics and the trauma the execution videos had inflicted on the nation.

"I was the very first administration official to talk publicly about our hostage policy," Frantz later recalled. "I thought it was important that we engage with the families in a public way, but the opposition was very strong." Officials from the State Department and the FBI tried to block Frantz's appearance and

sent several people to sit in the audience and report back about
every word he said.

In the fall of 2014, President Obama ordered a comprehensive
review of U.S. hostage policy. Lisa Monaco had seen the anger and
frustration from Diane and the hostage families. "I recommended
to the president that we had to really step back and figure out how
we could do better," Monaco recalled. Jen Easterly, who had been
the Senior Director for Counterterrorism on the National Security Council and the primary point of contact at the White House
for Diane following Jim's murder, urged Monaco to involve the
families in the review process. Monaco agreed.

Monaco convened the deputy secretaries of all the government agencies involved in hostage response. They decided
that the work should be led by the National Counterterrorism
Center, which was created following the September 11 attacks
to better coordinate intelligence and analyze terror threats. Lt.
General Bennet Sacolick, a former Delta Force commander and
the NCTC's director for strategic operational planning, was put
in charge of the effort.

The meetings took place in a secure conference room at the
NCTC headquarters in northern Virginia, outside Washington.
All the federal agencies involved in hostage policy and hostage response were represented—among them the FBI, the CIA,
the State Department, the Treasury Department, the Justice
Department, the Office of the Director of National Intelligence,
representatives from the Joint Chiefs of Staff, the Defense
Department, and the Defense Intelligence Agency. At first the
group was small enough to sit around a conference table. But
once the agencies realized what was at stake, "they sent more

people and more senior people and they had to open this removable wall and expand the room," recalled one participant.

The larger group split into four breakouts that met weekly to discuss government coordination, family engagement, intelligence sharing, and U.S. government policy. Hostage families, among them the Foleys, were invited to share their experiences. Brian Jenkins from the RAND Corporation briefed them about the history and evolution of U.S. hostage policy. David Bradley described his personal experience—and frustration—in supporting the families of Americans kidnapped overseas. European allies were invited to make presentations via videoconference, and some were consulted in person.

Participants heard how families were shunted from agency to agency without a clear point of contact; they heard how families were given conflicting messages about whether they faced legal jeopardy if they paid a ransom; they heard how rivalries between government agencies and departments had compromised the government's response.

In order to improve communication and coordination, the review team proposed the creation of a "fusion cell" made up of the different agencies that respond when a kidnapping occurs. Proximity, collegiality, and trust would improve information-sharing and ensure that the full resources of the government were brought to bear in resolving the cases. Ironically, the same rivalries that had crippled response played out in the room when the question of who would house the agency arose, the FBI or the State Department. Their differences were both philosophical and practical.

The FBI's authority derived from the fact that kidnapping, both in the United States and overseas, is a federal crime. But international kidnappings can also pose threats to U.S. strategic and diplomatic interests. Solutions may require diplomatic engagement. The State Department provides consular services to Americans abroad, and is therefore often a point of contact for hostage families. It has the relationships and local knowledge to mobilize governments and to carry out negotiations. Outside the United States, the FBI has far fewer resources and is generally represented by a small team or a single legal attaché. Their relationships tend to be with local law enforcement, which are sometimes corrupt or incompetent or both.

State Department officials told me that they prefer to take a flexible approach to resolving hostage cases while the FBI is more rigid. FBI agents told me precisely the opposite and noted that they had far more experience in dealing with victims and their families. In the end, the decision came down to practicalities. The FBI had the space to house the fusion cell, and its leadership was behind the effort. It also had a computer system in place that could provide access to operational intelligence.

The review also led to the creation of a second coordinating body within the NSC, the Hostage Response Group, which would provide "policy guidance" to the fusion cell. A family liaison officer, a new position created within the fusion cell, would participate and ensure that the views of the hostage families were represented. A third outcome from the review was the creation of a new position within the Office of the Director of National Intelligence to better coordinate intelligence. The hope was also that intelligence could be more readily declassified and shared with the families.

While the hostage policy review looked at the issues from a variety of perspectives, there was little debate around the no

140   concessions framework. "When we had the scoping discussions it became pretty clear that there was no interest, appetite, or voice in the room to address the no concessions policy," Lisa Monaco recalled. Instead, the conversation evolved. "It was like, we are sticking with the no concessions policy. But what does it mean?" noted one participant.

It was the job of the policy subgroup to figure that out. They pored over the language of NSPD-12, the prevailing policy directive signed by President Bush in 2002, and found the language lacked clarity. For example, the existing directive did not address communication. The new policy, codified in Presidential Policy Directive 30, or PPD-30, made clear that the "government may itself communicate with hostage-takers, their intermediaries, interested governments, and local communities, to attempt to secure the safe recovery of the hostage." The government would also be permitted to assist families in their private communication, to ensure they were not defrauded.

As the draft policy was circulated to review participants, David Bradley noted that there was no provision for a high-level U.S. government representative to do the kind of work he had done in the Foley and Padnos cases. A new position—the Special Presidential Envoy for Hostage Affairs, to be housed at the State Department—was created at his suggestion.

The night before the new policy was unveiled the hostage families were invited to a detailed briefing at the NCTC. The meeting, which was scheduled for three hours, lasted six. There were many questions, many raw emotions, and a good deal of skepticism. Diane Foley stood up to speak. "We hope that you will change," she said. "We will watch and see. I don't want to feel that my son died in vain. That I cannot accept."

At a ceremony the next morning, June 24, 2015, President Obama declared, "Our top priority is the safe and rapid recovery of American hostages," but quickly added, "I am reaffirming that the United States government will not make concessions, such as paying ransom, to terrorist groups holding American hostages." While expressing sympathy for the plight of the families, Obama noted that, "As president, I also have to consider our larger national security. I firmly believe that the United States government paying ransom to terrorists risks endangering more Americans and funding the very terrorism that we're trying to stop. And so I firmly believe that our policy ultimately puts fewer Americans at risk."

In his remarks, Obama also noted that "no family of an American hostage has ever been prosecuted for paying a ransom for the return of their loved ones. The last thing that we should ever do is to add to a family's pain with threats like that."

Following the president's announcement, U.S. officials and diplomats met with key allies to answers questions and address concerns. While American and British officials I spoke with said they did not raise any concerns directly, Tom Keatinge, who directs the Center for Financial Crime and Security Studies at the Royal United Services Institute, a leading London-based think tank, said that privately British officials perceived Obama's statement as a kink in the unified no concessions approach. "The announcement was a surprise here in London," Keatinge told me.

While British Crown Prosecutors have considerable discretion in choosing how to apply the law, the British government believed that any assurances should be communicated privately to the families rather than announced to the world.

142   There was also a lack of clarity about how far the commitment would extend. What about families or friends who contributed to a ransom payment or organized a crowdsourcing campaign? What about the insurance companies? What about the banks? Could they face legal jeopardy? What about security consultants who deliver the ransom? What about soliciting the support of a third government, like Qatar? To cite Doug Milne's preferred term, these remained gray areas.

  Meanwhile, global events exposed apparent contradictions in the application of the no concessions policy, undermining confidence in the depth of the U.S. commitment. In May 2014, Army Private Bowe Bergdahl was released in exchange for five Taliban prisoners held at the U.S. Naval Base in Guantanamo Bay, Cuba. The arduous negotiation that had led to the agreement had been hosted in Doha, and conducted via Qatari intermediaries. Qatar also agreed to accept the released Guantanamo prisoners. The controversy surrounding the release was exacerbated by the Obama administration's ham-handed communications. In an interview, National Security Advisor Susan Rice claimed Bergdahl had served with "honor and distinction" despite the fact that he had abandoned his unit. Her language infuriated many members of the U.S. military and their families who claimed that soldiers had been killed and wounded searching for Bergdahl after he walked off his base.

  President Obama publicly welcomed Bergdahl's family to the White House Rose Garden, treating the prisoner exchange not as an unpleasant but necessary concession to bring an American servicemember home, but rather a policy victory and cause for celebration. While the U.S. government would not make concessions for the return of an American civilian held by

the Taliban, the framework was different for Bergdahl. After all,
he was a member of the U.S. military captured when engaged in
a Congressionally authorized military action. He was thus considered a prisoner of war. Under the Geneva Conventions, which
govern the law of armed conflict, prisoner exchanges are specifically allowed. Besides, as one senior official noted, the Obama
administration had indicated it was not planning to hold prisoners in Guantanamo forever. If they were going to be released
at some point, why not get something in return?

While there was a legal basis and a rationale for the negotiations that led to the release of Bergdahl, the distinction was
utterly lost on the families of American hostages, not to mention members of the Islamic State. After Bergdahl was released,
Jim Foley's captors tormented him and the other American hostages, pointing to the Bergdahl negotiations as an example of
American perfidy, according to Federico Motka. In their email
exchanges the kidnappers of Kayla Mueller also cited the Bergdahl case to cast doubt on her family's claim that they were
negotiating on their own, without the support of the U.S. government, which would not make any concessions.

Then there was the Jason Rezaian case in Iran. Rezaian, the
Tehran correspondent for the *Washington Post*, was arrested
along with several other reporters, including his wife Yeganeh
Salehi, in July 2014. While the others were eventually released,
Rezaian was held for eighteen months, put on trial, and convicted of espionage. His case was used by hard line elements
within the Iranian government to put pressure on the more
moderate factions engaged in negotiating the nuclear agreement with the United States. Their leverage was that they could
scuttle any deal they did not like by keeping Rezaian in prison

and provoking a crisis with the U.S. News accounts, and officials with whom I spoke, reported that Rezaian's case was discussed on the sidelines of the nuclear negotiations between
Secretary of State John Kerry and his Iranian counterpart,
Mohammad Javad Zarif.

Soon after Rezaian was released from prison, on January 16,
2016, the U.S. delivered $400 million to Iran, which because of
U.S. sanctions had to be paid in cash. It was loaded onto wooden
pallets and put on an unmarked cargo plane. The funds had
been deposited in U.S. banks as escrow for an arms deal concluded under the Shah but the money was frozen following the
1979 Revolution. U.S. officials claimed that the money was not
ransom because it rightfully belonged to Iran. However, it was
used as leverage to secure Rezaian's release. U.S. officials made
the case that Iran may have been entitled to the money, but they
would not get it so long as Rezaian and three other Americans
were being unjustly imprisoned.

In June 2015, the White House announced the creation of
the Hostage Recovery Fusion Cell and the establishment of the
Family Engagement Team. Mike McGarrity, an eighteen-year
veteran of the FBI with extensive experience in counterterrorism, was named the director. His two deputies were from
the State Department and Department of Defense. McGarrity
served for a year and a half, and was replaced by Rob Saale in
March 2017. When I met with Saale at the end of 2017, he told me
he is willing to consider any approach to hostage recovery that
is "moral, ethical, and legal." He was in the process of assembling
an external advisory group made up of leading experts.

Families and others who have worked with the fusion cell
have been very positive and told me coordination and outreach

have improved dramatically under the new structure. But not
everyone is impressed. Terry Anderson, the former hostage
held for seven years in Lebanon, called the fusion cell an
expensive public relations exercise and "the fastest example of
bureaucratic empire-building I have ever seen in my life." Some
grumble that despite the new coordinating structure, intelligence is not being shared with the families.

In September 2015, veteran diplomat Jim O'Brien was
appointed as the first Special Presidential Envoy for Hostage
Affairs. O'Brien described his role as "representing the government in engaging with captors, with third parties, and the families" as well as participating in the high-level meetings at which
U.S. policy is decided.

"In bureaucratic terms it meant I always had a seat at the
table," O'Brien explained. His job, as he saw it, was to make
sure that the families had a voice at the top levels of government
and that hostage cases could be quickly escalated and brought to
the attention of leadership, as opposed to the situation described
by the Foleys in which their son's case languished for a year
before the government become engaged.

O'Brien's model for how to use U.S. influence to secure the
release of American hostages—his template—was taken from
Richard Holbrooke, the veteran U.S. diplomat who had negotiated the 1995 Bosnia peace accords. O'Brien, who was the
State Department lawyer assigned to Holbrooke, recalled the
peace negotiations which took place at the U.S. Air Force base
in Dayton, Ohio. For the first week of the negotiations, Holbrooke stonewalled Serbian leader Slobodan Milosevic, making
the case that the only way that Milosevic could demonstrate that
he was truly in control and thus a reliable negotiating partner

146   was to compel the Bosnian forces holding journalist David Rohde to release him. Rohde, at the time a correspondent for the *Christian Science Monitor,* had been taken captive while reporting on the Srebrenica massacre. The tactic cornered Milosevic; he felt compelled to demonstrate to Holbrooke that he was in charge. On November 9, 1995, Rohde was released. Less than two weeks later, the Dayton Peace Agreement was wrapped up.

During seventeen months in his position—until the end of the Obama administration—O'Brien dealt with about a hundred cases of U.S. citizens kidnapped abroad. Most involved short-lived criminal incidents in places like Mexico and Nigeria, but about three dozen were longer-term hostage situations, mostly related to armed conflict in places like Yemen. Rather than leave the hostage negotiations only on a separate track, O'Brien, channeling Holbrooke, sought to link the resolution of any hostage situation to the possibility of broader political dialogue. "My theory is that it's the best way to establish command and control," O'Brien noted. "Maybe you build confidence, maybe you don't. But you establish who's in charge." While he never faced a challenge as daunting as the mass kidnapping of Westerners by the Islamic State in Syria, O'Brien came to believe that "even the most nihilistic group reports to somebody, and so you're always looking for those pressure tactics."

O'Brien sought to push the limits of the no concessions policy following the Hostage Policy Review, looking for political solutions and taking the view that the "U.S. government has to be in the middle of these discussions." But there was one line that he could not cross—money. "Paying ransom is fine outside of designated terrorist groups," he noted, referring to the families of the hostages. "It's normal. It happens all the

time." But the matter is obviously more complicated when terrorist groups are involved. "During the 2014 period we left a
lot of families to figure out what was a legitimate demand, to
try to raise money, to try to pay it," O'Brien noted. "It's a complete failure of government to leave some poor family to sort
out how this is supposed to happen. The open question from
the policy perspective is what we would do if a family were to
say, 'we're paying, we need to make sure the money gets to the
right person.' In a normal K & R case, the government would
handle it all for the family. I feel the government should handle
terrorist cases the same way."

The Hostage Policy Review and the new structures that were
put in place came about in response to a genuine crisis. But governments are lumbering beasts, and they don't move unless
prodded. A good part of prodding came from Diane Foley.

But her drive to transform the landscape for American hostages and their families was not complete. Diane's next effort
was focused on establishing a nonprofit dedicated to providing
support and guidance to the victim's family.

During a trip to Europe in the spring of 2014, the Foleys
met with representatives from an organization called Hostage
UK. The nonprofit had been co-founded by Rachel Briggs in
2004 following the 1996 kidnapping of her uncle by the ELN
in Colombia. He was freed after seven months when a ransom
was paid by the Danish company that employed him, according
to news reports. Briggs, who was a college student at the time,
recalled feeling isolated and overwhelmed. Hostage UK helps
families understand the government bureaucracy and provides for their emotional and psychological needs. When Briggs

148   visited Washington later in 2014 she met with Diane and Jim's girlfriend, April. "We talked about what we were doing in the UK," Briggs recalled. "And Diane said something like that had to exist in the U.S."

Only a few weeks after Jim was killed, Diane and John called Briggs in London. "Do you want to do this?" Diane asked. "Then let's do it together." Diane helped secure a major grant from the Ford Foundation. She also made her own contribution through the James W. Foley Legacy Foundation, which had been established following Jim's death.

In September 2015, Briggs moved to Washington, D.C. By April 2016 Hostage U.S. had launched with a staff of two, and with a host of strategic partners ranging from law offices to financial advisors. Briggs assembled a roster of about a dozen volunteers who accompany hostage families to meetings and provide support and guidance on such basic matters as how to obtain power of attorney, access bank accounts when someone is in captivity, or deal with the inquiries of neighbors and friends. In its first year and a half, Hostage U.S. handled about fifty cases, a mix of terrorism-related, criminal kidnappings, and political detentions.

In early 2016, Diane directed an additional small grant to Hostage U.S., which allowed the organization to hire interns to comb through publicly reported cases, existing datasets, and other public records and assemble an inventory of hostage incidents going back to 2001. This data was provided to the New America Foundation, a leading Washington think tank which added its own research to carry out a systematic analysis of effectiveness of U.S. hostage policy. The New America study, launched

in January 2017 and entitled, "To Pay Ransom or Not to Pay
Ransom," concluded that "American hostages have suffered
disproportionately bad outcomes compared to other Western
hostages." Based on an analysis of the data, the study's authors
noted, "The United States' strict adherence to its no concessions
policy has also contributed to the failure of American efforts to
recover hostages. The no concessions policy is defended on the
basis that paying ransoms would create incentives for U.S. citizens to be kidnapped and that ransom payments finance terrorist groups. No clear evidence exists to support the claim that
Americans are targeted less often because of the no concessions
policy. On the other hand, there is strong evidence to suggest
that a no concessions policy puts hostages at greater risk once
abducted."

The New America study precipitated a public debate around
the no concessions framework and challenged the government to present better evidence to support its policy conclusions. With a few thousand dollars donated to Hostage U.S. to
support the organization of its data, Diane had helped shift the
national dialogue around a key issue of public policy. "Diane is
always pushing," acknowledged Peter Bergen, CNN's national
security analyst, a New America Foundation vice president, and
co-author of the study.

During the chaotic transition from Obama to President
Donald Trump, Lisa Monaco made a point of personally briefing
her successor as Homeland Security Advisor, Tom Bossert, on
the hostage policy review and the status of the pending cases.
She urged Bossert to give the issue focus and attention, and to
ensure that the families had someone in the White House they
could call on. Bossert met with the hostage families—including

150   the Foleys—as well as with cabinet members, with members of
        the Hostage Response Fusion Cell, and with a range of outside
        experts. "There were not a lot of policies from President Obama
        that I would accept without change, but the hostage policy is
        one of them, in part because it was created in consultation with
        the families," Bossert told me. After completing his assessment,
        he recommended to President Trump that the Obama hostage
        policy and the newly created structures be maintained. Presi-
        dent Trump accepted the recommendation without comment,
        according to Bossert.

        In fact, in his first year in office President Trump took a
        strong personal interest in the fate of Americans held overseas,
        both hostages and those wrongfully detained by governments.

        In October 2017, U.S. officials told Pakistani authorities
        they had located a group of hostages being held by the Taliban.
        An American woman, Caitlan Coleman, her Canadian husband,
        Joshua Boyle, and their children were being transported by car
        to a new safe house. The family had been held hostage for five
        years by members of the Haqqani network. Unless they acted,
        the Pakistanis were told, the U.S. would send a Seal Team which
        was on standby to execute a rescue. The Pakistanis managed to
        stop the car and free the hostages.

        Brian Jenkins calls hostage-taking "political dynamite." If
        not carefully managed, a single hostage incident can blow up
        an entire administration. At times President Obama seemed to
        be so focused on executing the policy—which was intended to
        deprive terror groups of funding—that he failed to fully con-
        sider the emotional dimensions of the hostage issue. Trump,
        on the other hand, appears uninterested in the issue's strategic
        complexity.

But Trump has quickly grasped the political implications and recognized that if he can get an American home it will be a political win that will resonate with his America First base. Hostage families say they are pleased with the attention that President Trump has given the issue. On the other hand, Trump has demonstrated a disregard bordering on contempt for the kind of local knowledge and relationships that come from having a robust and seasoned diplomatic corps. This kind of support is vital in any complex international hostage situation.

Epilogue

In March 2017, I visited Diane and John Foley at their home in Rochester, New Hampshire. We spent several hours talking about their experience dealing with U.S. officials; the evolution of hostage policy; and the varying approaches to hostage-taking around the world. Diane had made soup in an electric slow cooker, which she served along with fresh bread. By the early afternoon clouds were building up and a late spring snowstorm was moving in. Diane promised to make introductions to members of her vast network, and over the next few weeks she followed up. On June 29, Diane wrote to Federico Motka and another former hostage held alongside Jim, urging them to speak with me. "Jim's Legacy Foundation is seeking to bring the truth to light on this issue," Diane wrote. "May God bless you both in every way."

Thus began an assignment that brought me face-to-face with former hostages, their families, government officials, intelligence officers, policymakers, security consultants, researchers, and academics. Not surprisingly, I heard a wide variety of

views on the question of whether governments should ever
pay ransom to terrorists. Over time, I found there were three
frameworks through which people tended to view the issue.
There were those who saw it as an ethical question, those who
saw it as a policy dilemma, and those who saw it as a political
problem.

Those who saw it as a matter of ethics came down on both
sides of the issue. Some claimed it was morally wrong for a government to allow a citizen to die when they could be saved by
paying ransom. Others, that it was wrong for a government to
give money to terrorists even if it was to save the life of one of
its own citizens. In 2017, Jeffrey Howard, a lecturer at University College London, published an essay entitled "Kidnapped:
The Ethics of Paying Ransom" in which he agreed with both of
these views. Howard argued that it's unethical for a government
to withhold ransom if the motivation is to deter future kidnappings. This is because the harm caused by refusing to pay (the
death of the hostage) is greater than the harm caused by paying
(the possibility of additional kidnapping victims, who would
also presumably be ransomed). However, the ethical considerations shift if the intent of the government is to deprive terror
groups of funding that could be used to kill thousands. Howard
concluded that "those who pay ransoms to unjust organizations
become reluctant accomplices to those unjust activities" and
that therefore "the impermissibility of paying ransoms depends
in part on the evil the ransom payments fund." This moral prohibition applies equally to states and families.

Of course in real life families looking to save their loved
ones are not going to be overly concerned with abstract moral
arguments. Likewise, governments don't operate on the basis

154 of ethics, although lawmakers and policymakers may be influenced by such considerations. People I spoke with who looked at the issue from a policy perspective tended to frame their arguments slightly differently, citing pragmatic considerations. Refusing to pay ransom deters future kidnappings, making all citizens safer. Depriving terror organizations of funding ensures these groups don't have the funds to carry out operations targeting our citizens. However, effective policies tend to be based on solid data and research that demonstrate specific actions are likely to produce specific results. The evidence to support the argument that refusing to pay ransom deters future kidnapping is very thin. Research carried out by the RAND Corporation in the 1970s and recent studies from West Point and the New America Foundation all concluded there was insufficient evidence to demonstrate this correlation. Only a 2016 study published in the *European Journal of Political Economy* found a deterrent effect.

Those who approach the problem from a political perspective tend to believe that there are too many variables for the question to be addressed through a policy framework. Because European governments that pay ransom deny doing so they can't publicly justify their actions. But a variety of people I spoke with, from former French hostages to Spanish journalists, said they wanted and expected their country's leadership to make a decision based on the specific circumstances of each case. Framing the decision to pay or not as fundamentally political allows for greater flexibility, but also means that public sentiment rather than strategic consideration is often the deciding factor.

Governments of course have a legitimate interest in seeking to deprive kidnappers of the benefits of their actions. But the victims of kidnappings have a right to seek the return of their loved ones. Phrases such as "we don't negotiate with terrorists" or "we make no concessions to terrorists" are political slogans. As Federico Motka noted, your principle should not necessarily be your policy. And as the Royal United Services Institute study determined, a strict no concessions policy may even have a perverse effect, increasing the amount of money going to terrorists while raising the likelihood that hostages will be killed.

Of course, a strict no concessions policy should work perfectly in some kind of political laboratory in which no ransom is ever paid. This would undermine the economic logic of the crime. But it will never happen. Families will find a way to pay. Businesses cannot be expected to walk away and let their employees die. And many European governments, having done the political math, are willing to shell out. The most effective way for hostage takers to put pressure on the governments that do pay is to murder one of the hostages. The disparate policies make the decision easy. Osama Bin Laden's strategic advice to Al Qaeda was to kill the least valuable hostage. In the current environment that's likely to be an American or a Brit.

The back and forth between no concessions countries and the countries that pay has not been productive and has not created a consensus. The international legal framework—codified in the January 2014 Security Council Resolution—has not led to a notable reduction in the willingness of governments to pay ransom and to the extent that it is ignored it actually undermines the credibility of the international legal regime.

If it's not possible to forge a global consensus around no concessions, and if a mixed environment—in which some countries pay ransom and others don't—produces the worst possible

156   outcomes, then the logical conclusion is to try the opposite approach. That means recognizing that governments will make concessions, and developing a recognized framework for decisionmaking. Fortunately, one already exists. It's called national security. This is the prism through which most modern nation states make difficult decisions about how to deploy power in defense of their citizens and their interests. Different countries obviously have different conceptions of national security, and these will also vary over time. In many instances, depending on the country and circumstances, paying ransom for the return of a national citizen kidnapped abroad will undermine national security. This is true for the many reasons outlined by British and American officials, including the fact that ransom payments will go to terrorist groups.

But there are other circumstances in which the payment of ransom enhances national security by depriving terrorists of a victim for an execution video or, in the formulation of Florence Aubenas, publicly affirming the regard in which a country holds its citizens at a time when this is being challenged. The ability of terror groups to use modern technologies to disseminate propaganda videos greatly changes the calculation. From ISIS's twisted perspective, the videos they made of hostages being beheaded or burned in cages greatly increased their visibility, strengthened their "brand," and aided their recruitment.

From a pure negotiating standpoint, adopting a public posture of "we don't negotiate with terrorists" is a terrible opening gambit. President Nixon discovered this when he first articulated the policy in 1973. It insults the hostage-takers and undermines the value of the hostages, which is all that keeps them alive. Instead the best posture is one that I call strategic ambiguity, in which governments give no indication about their intentions. To the extent that a government speaks publicly at all about hostage policy it's probably best to limit the statement to bland expressions like, "our approach is to do all we reasonably can to support the families." Preserving the life of the hostage, improving trust between families and governments, and creating an atmosphere in which active negotiations are possible has many benefits. It can aid with intelligence-gathering: information that can be used to plan a military rescue should the opportunity present itself, recover the ransom, or bring the perpetrators to justice.

If there is a recognition that national security may require governments in certain situations to seek the release of hostages through the payment of ransom then the question becomes, how should this be achieved? The worst approach is the one practiced by many European countries in which they engage in direct negotiations with the hostage-takers. As Doug Milne notes, governments can't plead poverty, so once hostage-takers realize they are dealing with a government the demands will almost certainly increase. This inflates the market itself, meaning the amount of money flowing to terrorists actually increases; criminal groups demand more; and families that must fend for themselves struggle to come up with ever larger ransoms. Farming out payments to third-party governments creates some deniability but also fuels the market. When Qatar and Oman decide to intervene and pay ransom, it's for their own strategic reasons, generally to strengthen their relationship with European powers and to gain influence and leverage. Having determined a strategic opportunity exists, these countries are unlikely to strike a tough deal. A million

158   dollars plus or minus is not going to make a difference to a country like Qatar but could make a big difference in the hostage market. (In April 2017, Qatar paid hundreds of millions of dollars to a Shia militia and a range of intermediaries to free twenty-five members of a royal falcon hunting party taken hostage in southern Iraq.)

Moreover, and as Didier Le Bret argues, the visible involvement of the political leadership sends a terrible message that undermines negotiations and highlights weakness and vulnerability. The ritual of presidents meeting freed hostages at the airport must stop. It's a crude form of political opportunism that exploits a moment of supreme vulnerability for the hostage to secure a photo op that ultimately benefits the politicians. For the sake of the hostages and their families, homecomings should be quiet affairs, outside the spotlight.

Public mobilizations and media campaigns are an effective tool for putting pressure on governments that are not acting in the best interest of the hostages. But they also complicate negotiations and can fuel the worst instincts of national leaders, which is to use the hostage negotiations for their own political gain. For this reason, such efforts must be managed carefully. "People want to react, whether it makes sense or not," noted Christophe Deloire, the head of Reporters Without Borders, describing the days and weeks after a hostage is taken. "But the question of strategy is really important. These things can last a really long time and we need a plan. The target is the authorities but it is also the guys who hold the hostage to say to them, 'this person is precious.' It would not make sense to kill him or her. And sometimes we can send a message to the hostages themselves, speaking through the media."

Once it is acknowledged that under certain circumstances
and conditions governments will pay, it opens the door for
everyone to work together to address the real problem, which
is that they pay too much. Governments, families, employers,
insurance companies—everyone involved in hostage recovery
shares a common interest in reducing the amount of the ransom.
An acknowledgment of the shortcomings of the current approach
allows a discussion about how to reduce the amount of ransom
payment to be more productive and more direct. Research from
various studies points to the same conclusion. Hostage-taking
is largely opportunistic and unrelated to the hostage policies of a
particular country. But those policies are highly relevant to outcomes. Large ransom payments drive up the market and make
the crime more attractive. Holding and keeping a hostage for an
extended period of time takes resources. Reducing the amount or
ransom will not eliminate the crime, but if it reduces the return
on investment it might make the crime less attractive. It will certainly ensure that fewer resources go to terrorists.

In order to keep ransom payments down, governments that
choose to pay ransom must hide their involvement from the
hostage-takers. This can be best accomplished by privatizing
the negotiation process. This is already done in criminal cases
when a K & R policy is activated and a security consultant is
brought on. Increasingly, it is being done in France, which in the
last several years began licensing professional hostage negotiators. The quality of security consultants obviously varies con-
siderably. It is also unsavory to see private companies profiting
from a family's misery by helping them deliver money to criminals. Yet it must be acknowledged that the industry has a record
of success.

160   What negotiators can do effectively is front for the government, putting themselves forward as family representatives. If
the hostage-takers make political demands, the negotiator can
credibly say they are not speaking for the government and try
to push the kidnappers toward a financial resolution. Governments should work to expand access to K & R policies to those
operating in high-risk environments, including freelance journalists, independent aid workers, and even adventure tourists,
as outlined in Chapter Four. Such efforts can be combined with
initiatives to educate vulnerable groups about the risk of undertaking such travel without proper preparations.

However, if a kidnapping occurs and the family does not
have access to a professional private negotiator because they do
not have K & R insurance, then governments should find a way
to provide this support. This could be done in cases with clear
national security implications, through a government program
that compensates security firms. Governments have a clear and
compelling interest in ensuring that no family is negotiating
directly with a terrorist group without adequate support. This
approach requires that the regulation of the K & R industry be
relaxed to eliminate the distinction between criminal and terrorist groups—which is, in any case, often arbitrary.

Eliminating the prohibition on paying money to proscribed
groups would mean that criminal and terrorist cases would
be handled in the same way. A private negotiator would support the families and seek to negotiate a monetary settlement.
The families or the employers would be responsible for raising
the funds. The government would monitor the negotiations,
ensure the families were not defrauded, and in some cases deliver
the money. They would also engage in intelligence-gathering

that might help them plan and organize a rescue, in the rare cases where they are warranted, or apprehend the kidnappers following the delivery of the ransom. Having a framework in which governments recognize and acknowledge that such arrangements exist and are necessary could improve information-sharing and trust among intelligence agencies since countries that support the payment of ransom would no longer have to hide their involvement from those that do not.

There would be one fundamental variable. In national security cases, families seeking to raise money to pay a ransom might suddenly receive a donation or donations from a concerned individual, or a front company, or a local NGO. The families would not necessarily know where this money came from. Such a system would allow those governments that seek to pay to do so quietly, without drawing attention to their involvement and increasing the demands of the hostage-takers.

This approach recognizes that kidnapping and hostage-taking is a tactic of war and cannot be eliminated. Trying to end kidnapping by blocking the payment of ransom is like trying to wipe out car bombing by banning the sale of gasoline. Brian Jenkins found no correlation between government refusal to pay ransom and a decline in hostage-taking in a particular environment. The only way to end political kidnapping, in Jenkin's view, is to neutralize the groups that are carrying it out. This can be done through political settlements, as occurred in Colombia and Lebanon; by expanding security, as was done in response to Somali piracy; or by military means, as occurred with Sendero Luminoso in Peru. But it is always a long process.

The underlying principle is that each hostage situation is different and each hostage crisis is different. Hostage policy

162   tends to be made in response to the last crisis, and does not anticipate effectively what might be coming down the road. That is why maximum flexibility should be the goal.

Each country's media is likely to respond based on its practices and traditions. In France, where unions are stronger and the media tends to be more activist, media organizations have come together to develop joint campaigns and put pressure on the French government. In Spain, there is a consensus around limiting reporting in active hostage cases. In the U.S., a tradition of independence and a growing polarization make that kind of solidarity difficult. But all over the world, the media can agree on certain principles.

Complete "blackouts" of kidnapping cases are often unhelpful; they allow the hostage-takers to control communication and can also obscure areas of growing risk, as occurred in northern Syria in 2013. By the same token, campaigning, crusading, or sensational coverage can often complicate negotiations and should be avoided in active cases. Reporting the size of the ransom payment can also be problematic. I've seen two cases in which inaccurate media reports of inflated ransoms caused the hostage-takers to conclude incorrectly that a portion of the ransom had been siphoned off and to take out their frustration on other hostages. Journalists should avoid using images or videos disseminated by terror groups, as the use of such images amplifies terror propaganda. Keeping such images off social media is more challenging. Steps taken by Twitter to investigate and remove users who disseminate terror content have helped, as has the deployment of more sophisticated algorithms. But it's tremendously distressing that a Google search for David Haines turns up images of his decapitated body. No one has yet come up with a perfect formula on how to limit the availability of such images on social media without undermining free speech.

Finally, governments have a strategic interest in ensuring that families feel supported. This prevents the hostage-takers from using the murder of a hostage to exploit the perceived indifference of the victim's government as a way of amplifying their own propaganda. As the Spanish experience shows, families that feel supported by their governments are less likely to launch media campaigns, which can complicate negotiations and delay a resolution.

A no concessions policy is only credible if governments are willing to let hostages die to make the point that they will never give in. A government that expects its citizens to make that kind of sacrifice should only do so based on incontrovertible evidence that many other lives will be saved. The no concessions policy does not meet that standard. It's time for a new approach. No one should have to die for a policy that isn't working.

Putting words to paper is necessarily a solitary endeavor. But it is only a small part of writing a book. Most of the rest takes friends, assistants, colleagues, and family. This book would not have been possible without the help of many.

Let me start by expressing a huge debt of gratitude to my researchers, an amazing team who have not (yet!) been introduced. In the U.S., Courtney Glenn Vinopal; in France, Laure Fourquet; and in Spain, Guillermo D. Olmo. All three are experts in their own right. Each made a huge contribution through reporting, translating, analyzing, summarizing, transcribing, and organizing.

I am inspired to work every day with such a dedicated, talented and committed group of people at the Committee to Protect Journalists. I'm indebted to my CPJ colleagues who generously shared information, insights, contacts, and local knowledge. Colin Pereira, CPJ's self-described "safety guy," is an expert on kidnapping and ransom. He provided informed criticism and introduced me to his vast network, including Doug Milne, whose account is featured in Chapter Three. Colin was also a reader, as was Jason Stern, a former CPJ Middle East Program researcher and Syria expert. I'm grateful to John Otis, CPJ's Andes Correspondent and author of the seminal book on kidnapping in Colombia, *Law of the Jungle.* Special thank yous as well to CPJ's Deputy Executive Director Robert Mahoney, who picked up the slack while I was on the road, and to my assistant at CPJ, Jake Rothenberg, who helped me keep everything straight.

Former CPJ chair Sandy Rowe could not have been more supportive. She encouraged me to pursue this project, approved

166   time away to research and write, and was the first to read this manuscript. Her editorial insights guided me out of more than a few literary dead ends. I am also grateful to Kathleen Carroll, who replaced Sandy as chair in the summer of 2017, and has led CPJ with wisdom and determination.

It has been an incredible experience to work with Columbia Global Reports, which is playing a critical role at the intersection of journalism and global affairs. Every step of the process was refreshing, streamlined, and thoughtful. It's been a treat to work with the editorial team of Nick Lemann and Jimmy So. I am grateful to CGR publisher Camille McDuffie along with my agent Stephanie Steiker, who made it all happen.

I'd like to extend a very special thank you to my friend Eric Siblin, who provided detailed feedback on early drafts. Peter Bergen and Christopher Mellon at the New America Foundation generously shared their extensive research and Chris took the time to walk me through the numbers. Thanks as well to others who shared ideas, contacts, or expertise. These include (in no particular order) Doug Frantz, Kati Marton, Rachel Briggs, Phil Balboni, Charlie Sennott, Nick Quested, Sebastian Junger, Martin Morgan, Lisa Monaco, Jen Easterly, Jim O'Brien, Jessica Bohrer, Gary Noesner, David Rohde, Kristen Mulvihill, Christophe Deloire, Ali Soufan, and Josh Geltzer. Thank you as well to the many other experts who spoke with me but asked not to be cited in these pages.

I wrote this book because Diane Foley challenged me to question my assumptions. She did more than that. She recommended me to her vast network. I am so grateful to the many people who shared their experiences, some of them terrible, and deposited in me the trust that I would tell their stories with

compassion. I hope that I have met those expectations. I wish   167
to single out Federico Motka, Mike Haines, Florence Aubenas,
Didier Francois, Javier Espinosa, and Mónica Prieto. My special
thanks as well to Paula and Ed Kassig, and to Art and Shirley
Sotloff.

I could also not be more grateful for the attention of Emily
Lenzer and Aretae Wyler from *The Atlantic,* who gave hours of
their time to make sure I got the details right (and if I didn't, the
errors are mine).

Finally, there is my family. I include them last only because
they are the foundation upon which all else is built. A book is
an obsession, so living with a writer—especially one with a
full-time job—requires patience and love. This I received in
spades. My daughters Ruby and Lola also provided thoughtful
criticism and informed insights. They were there for me when I
needed to work through tough problems. My wife Ingrid toler-
ated my absences and managed my frustrations. She even edited
my chapters. For the twenty years of our marriage she has been
both my soulmate and biggest supporter. She is the best partner
any writer could have.

CHAPTER ONE

Florence Aubenas's *The Night Cleaner* reveals the brutal working conditions endured by France's working class.

Christian Chesnot and Georges Malbrunot's *Nos Très Chers Emirs* explores the complex relationship between France and its allies in the Persian Gulf.

Dorothee Moisan's *Rançons: le Business des Otages* looks at the business of hostage-taking, with a particular focus on the Kidnapping and Ransom (K&R) industry.

The Pearl Project was an initiative of Georgetown University that confirmed details surrounding the death of Daniel Pearl, including his killer, Khalid Sheikh Mohammed.

Mariane Pearl's *A Mighty Heart* tells the story of Daniel Pearl's kidnapping and killing through the eyes of his wife.

Terry Anderson's *Den of Lions* is the definitive personal account of the Lebanese hostage crisis. See also, *The Hostage's Daughter,* by Sulome Anderson, a personal account of the toll that Anderson's kidnapping took on his family and his daughter's quest for answers.

CHAPTER TWO

Josh Hammer's *The Bad Ass Librarians of Timbuktu* tells the story of Abdel Kader Haidara's mission to rescue centuries-old Arabic texts from Mali after Al Qaeda seized control of the country in 2012.

Jay Badahur's *The Pirates of Somalia* goes inside the world of Somali pirates, drawing upon interviews about their lives, spending, and deadly missions.

170   Daniele Mastrogiacomo's *Days of Fear* is a firsthand account of the
days the author spent in captivity of the Taliban, who kidnapped
him and his driver in Afghanistan in 2007.

CHAPTER THREE

In *A House in the Sky,* Amanda Lindhout recounts the 460
harrowing days that she spent in captivity after being kidnapped in
Somalia.

A Rope and a Prayer is the account of *New York Times* reporter David
Rohde, who was kidnapped while reporting in Afghanistan. It also
features chapters from Rohde's wife Kristen Mulvihill, who worked
tirelessly for his release.

Gabriel García Márquez's *News of a Kidnapping* is the definitive
chronicle of the wave of kidnappings carried out by Medellin Cartel
in the early 1990s. The victims included Maruja Pachón, Diana
Turbay, and *El Tiempo* editor Francisco "Pacho" Santos, who would
later be elected the country's vice president.

Michael Scott Moore's *The Desert and the Sea: 977 Days Captive on
the Somali Pirate Coast* is both a haunting personal memoir and a
reflection on the nature of Somali piracy.

Ann Hagedorn Auerback's *Ransom: The Untold Story of
International Kidnapping* details the rise in international
kidnappings since the Cold War.

Judith Tebbutt's *A Long Walk Home* is a first-person account of her
kidnapping at the hands of Somali pirates.

In *Impossible Odds*, aid worker Jessica Buchanan and her husband,
Erik Landemalm, recall Buchanan's months spent in captivity in
Somalia, and Landemalm's efforts to win her release.

CHAPTER FOUR

John Otis's *Law of the Jungle* chronicles stories of kidnapping and drug trafficking in the South American jungles.

Even Silence Has an End is Ingrid Betancourt's firsthand account of her six and half years held by FARC militants in the Colombian jungle

Juan Zarate's *Treasury's War: The Unleashing of a New Era of Financial Warfare* details the U.S. administration's efforts to leverage financial power in order to hold powerful regimes accountable.

547 Jours is Hervé Guesquière's account of his time spent in captivity in Afghanistan.

Russel D. Buhite's *Lives at Risk: Hostages and Victims in American Foreign Policy* provides a history of the U.S. response to kidnapping and terrorism.

In the Presence of My Enemies, by Gracia Burnham with Dean Merrill, is an account of Burnham's life as a hostage of the Abu Sayyaf, and the rescue effort that cost the life of her husband.

CHAPTER FIVE

Loretta Napoleoni's *Merchants of Men* looks at the rise of kidnapping and refugee trafficking among extremist groups that have gained a hold on the Western world post-9/11.

In *Hunting Season*, James Harkin investigates James Foley's kidnapping and killing, as well as the two dozen other ISIS hostages taken around the same time as Jim.

Javier Lesaca's *Armas de Seduccion* is an examination of the digital tactics used by ISIS to recruit its most vulnerable new members.

In *El país de las alma rotas*, Javier Espinosa and Mónica G. Preito
detail their days covering the Syrian Civil War, followed by the
kidnapping of Javier.

The ISIS Hostage is Puk Damsgård's account of the kidnapping of
Daniel Rye.

Lawrence Wright's *The Terror Years* is a collection of the author's
reporting on the Middle East, including five families whose
children were kidnapped by ISIS.

Janine DiGiovanni's *The Morning They Came For Us* provides a
firsthand look at the horrors lived by Syrians experiencing the
Civil War each day.

Jonathan Powell's *Talking to Terrorists: How to End Armed Conflict*
examines the art of negotiating with extremist organizations.

CHAPTER SIX

In *The Trade*, Jere Van Dyk reexamines his kidnapping and eventual
release in Afghanistan, and probes the shadowy world of hostage
negotiations.

NOTES

INTRODUCTION

15   On kidnapping in Mexico: https://www.washingtonpost.com/ world/the_americas/kidnappings- in-mexico-surge-to-the-highest- number-on-record/2014/08/15/ 3f8ee2d2-1e6e-11e4-82f9-2cd6 fa8da5c4_story.html?utm_term= .af22822fa868.

16   According to a December 2015 study: "Analyses of Kidnapping Across Time and Among Jihadist Organizations," Seth Loertscher and Daniel Milton (The Combating Terrorism Center at West Point), December 2015.

CHAPTER ONE

20 Most of this chapter was reported in July 2017, while I was based in Paris. During this period I interviewed Florence Aubenas, Georges Malbrunot, Laurent Combalbert, Didier Le Bret, Hala Kodmani, and many others who asked to speak on background. Aubenas declined to speak in detail about the circumstances of her own kidnapping and so the account is based on news reports and other public sources, as cited below.

20   On the kidnapping of Florence Aubenas: https://www.theguardian .com/media/2005/jan/14/ Iraqandthemedia.iraq; http:// www.aljazeera.com/archive/2005/ 06/2008410115226711527.html.

21   On activities carried out in support of Aubenas: http://www .liberation.fr/courrier/2005/04/21/ que-tous-les-moyens-soient-mis- en-oeuvre_517152.

22   Aubenas pleads to Didier Julia for help: https://www.theguardian .com/world/2005/mar/02/ pressandpublishing.media.

22   Didier Julia told to butt out of DGSE activity: http://www .liberation.fr/evenement/2005/06/ 13/cinq-mois-de-tractations_523153.

22   Details of Didier François's bureau in Baghdad: http://www .europe1.fr/international/aubenas- didier-francois-est-un-journaliste- de-plain-pied-1603201.

24   *Times of London* on ransom payment: https://www.thetimes .co.uk/article/how-dollar45m- secretly-bought-freedom-of- foreign-hostages-j8vlt00znzx.

25   Global rise in kidnapping: https://worldview.stratfor.com/ article/global-rise-kidnappings- ransom.

26 The kidnapping data from 1970s to 2013 is drawn from the Global Terrorism Database (available at http://www.start.umd.edu/gtd/).

26   Description of political kidnapping in in the 1970s and '80s from *Ransom: The Untold Story of International Kidnapping* by Ann Hagedorn Auerbach (New York: Henry Holt, 1998). See also "Does the U.S. No Concessions Policy Deter Kidnappings of Americans?" Brian Michael Jenkins, RAND, 2018 https://www.rand.org/pubs/ perspectives/PE277.html.

27 **Rise of interconnected Jihadi movements after 9/11:** See "Held Hostage: Analyses of Kidnappings Across Time and Across Jihadist Organizations." https://ctc.usma .edu/wp-content/uploads/2015/12/ Held-Hostagereportc2.pdf

27 **Daniel Pearl's kidnapping and killing:** I was involved in responding to the Pearl kidnapping in my CPJ role and wrote about it in *The New Censorship: Inside the Global Battle for Media Freedom* (New York: Columbia University Press, 2014). See also *A Mighty Heart* and The Pearl Project, both referenced in Additional Reading. For a summary of the Pearl Project's conclusion see below. http://www.washingtonpost.com/ wp-dyn/content/article/2011/01/20/ AR2011012000057.html

27 **Nick Berg kidnapping and killing:** http://abcnews.go.com/ Archives/video/nick-berg-beheaded- iraq-2004-10062350.

28 **Thomas Hedghammer's FFI report:** https://www.ffi.no/no/ Rapporter/04-03105.pdf.

28 **2017 New America study:** https://na-production.s3 .amazonaws.com/documents/ hostage-paper-final.pdf.

29 **2003 German ransom payment of 5 million euros:** https:// www.nytimes.com/2014/07/30/ world/africa/ransoming-citizens- europe-becomes-al-qaedas-patron .html.

29 **Italian aid workers freed:** https://www.theguardian.com/ world/2004/sep/29/italy.iraq

29 **"During a decade-long period, from 1982 to 1992, cells linked to Hezbollah, Islamic Jihad, and ultimately the revolutionary regime in Iran, took more than a hundred hostages in Lebanon":** Robert Worley, *Orchestrating the Instruments of Power*, https://books .google.com/books?id=yuDBAw AAQBAJ&pg=PA204&lpg=PA 204&dq=lebanon+hostage+crisis +1982+1992&source=bl&ots=j1G W4Z6bwx&sig=g-nkHiqvCaUPi- 1BBgm5i5FlU_Q&hl=en&sa=X&ved= 0ahUKEwjcttyaoNXYAhWnQt8 KHXhYDEsQ6AEIajAN#v=onepage &q=lebanon%20hostage%20crisis% 201982%201992&f=false.

29 **"Among them was the U.S. journalist Terry Anderson, and the British envoy Terry Waite":** http:// www.cnn.com/2016/02/09/world/ terry-anderson-hostage-rewind/ index.html; http://www.telegraph .co.uk/men/thinking-man/terry- waite-i-spent-five-years-as-a- hostage-in-beirut-but-i-ne/.

29 **Jean-Paul Kauffmann and Michel Seurat held captive in Lebanon:** http://www.nytimes.com/ 1988/05/11/world/beirut-captivity- a-frenchman-s-story.html.

30 **French hostages freed in Beirut:** http://www.nytimes .com/1988/05/05/world/french- hostages-freed-in-beirut-boon- for-chirac.html.

34 *Times of London* **on ransom payment:** https://www .thetimes.co.uk/article/how-dollar 45m-secretly-bought-freedom-of- foreign-hostages-j8vlt00znzx.

35   **Ransom demand for Christian Chesnot and Georges Malbrunot:** http://www.telegraph.co.uk/news/worldnews/middleeast/iraq/1470558/Paris-panic-after-journalists-kidnapped-in-Iraq.html.

36   **Qatar's ties to terrorist groups:** http://www.bbc.com/news/world-middle-east-40246734.

38   **AQIM's pledge to be "a bone in the throat of American and French crusaders."** https://www.longwarjournal.org/archives/2013/08/the_press_quickly_learned_that.php.

38   **"The number of French nationals abducted overseas quintupled from 11 to 59 per year between between 2004 and 2008":** https://www.msf-crash.org/en/publications/saving-lives-and-staying-alive-humanitarian-security-age-risk-management.

38   **Kidnapping of Pierre Camatte:** http://www.lemonde.fr/afrique/article/2013/03/18/otages-la-france-ne-veut-plus-payer_1849987_3212.html.

38   **Eduoard Guillaud's comments on Spain:** https://www.google.com/url?q=https://wikileaks.org/plusd/cables/10PARIS30_a.html&sa=D&ust=1514567703988000&usg=AFQjCNFgsfIKCBpxUqc5506ZxRiRuladSg.

39   **Camatte released:** http://www.france24.com/en/20100223-

al-qaeda-releases-kidnapped-frenchman-pierre-camatte.

39   **Kidnapping of Hervé Ghesquière and Stephane Taponier:** http://www.lemonde.fr/international/article/2012/09/21/le-livre-de-l-ancien-otage-herve-ghesquiere-ravive-la-polemique-avec-l-armee_1763671_3210.html; http://www.lemonde.fr/idees/article/2010/06/29/herve-ghesquiere-et-stephane-taponier-nous-devons-parler-d-eux-chaque-jour_1380291_3232.html.

39   **Ransom paid to Taliban for release of Ghesquière and Taponier:** https://www.thedailybeast.com/talibans-french-hostages-how-they-were-freed.

CHAPTER TWO

41   I interviewed General Sanz Roldán in the CNI headquarters outside Madrid on July 17, 2017. Most of the interview was on background. I have included only a limited number of quotes that he agreed to put on the record. I made a follow-up visit to the CNI in October 2017.

41   **Appointment of General Félix Sanz Roldán:** https://www.cni.es/en/biographicdetailsofthesecretaryofstatedirector/.

41   **"CNI had been wracked by allegations of fraud":** http://www.nytimes.com/2004/03/17/world/bombings-madrid-election-outcome-spain-grapples-with-notion-that-terrorism.html.

176   42   "deployment of Spanish troops in Iraq was opposed by 90 percent of the Spanish public": http://www.cnn.com/2003/WORLD/europe/03/29/sprj.irq.spain/.

42   "Zapatero waited only one day after taking office": https://www.theguardian.com/world/2004/mar/15/spain.iraq.

42   Condoleezza Rice's comment to Fox News: http://www.nytimes.com/2004/04/19/world/spanish-premier-orders-soldiers-home-from-iraq.html.

42   Altercation between Donald Rumsfeld and Spanish Minister of Defense: http://www.nytimes.com/2004/05/07/world/spanish-premier-says-troops-will-not-return-to-iraq.html.

42   Appointment by Zapatero as head of the Estado Mayor: http://www.elmundo.es/elmundo/2004/06/25/espana/1088122047.html.

43   *Alakrana* held hostage by Somali pirates: https://www.reuters.com/article/us-somalia-piracy-incidents-factbox/factbox-ships-held-by-somali-pirates-idUSTRE5A83KF20091109.

43   "about four hundred nautical miles northwest of the Seychelles": http://www.lavanguardia.com/politica/20091117/53826265705/el-secuestro-del-alakrana-uno-de-los-diez-mas-largos-sufridos-en-el-indico.html.

43   "operating out of a 'mother ship'": http://news.bbc.co.uk/2/hi/africa/8364530.stm.

43   "Two smaller skiffs carrying thirteen pirates": https://elpais.com/diario/2009/10/04/espana/1254607207_850215.html.

43   "toward the Somali city of Harare": http://cadenaser.com/ser/2009/10/04/espana/1254613812_850215.html.

43   Crew members aboard the *Alakrana:* http://www.nytimes.com/2009/11/07/world/europe/07spain.html.

44   I interviewed General Julio Rodríguez in Madrid on July 19; I spoke to Congresswoman and former Minister of International Cooperation Soraya Rodríguez on July 20. I spoke with *El Pais* reporter José María Irujo by phone on July 31. I spoke with Alain Juillet on July 4 and Didier Le Bret on July 27, both in Paris. I interviewed Jamal Osman by phone on July 21. Former U.S. Ambassador Vicki Huddleston is now retired and lives in ew Mexico. I spoke with her by phone on November 9, 2017.

44   "reportedly for a ransom of $1.2 million": http://www.abc.net.au/news/2008-04-27/spanish-fishing-boat-freed-for-128m/2417098.

44   On the prowess of Basque fishermen: See *Cod: A Biography of the Fish that Changed the World* by Mark Kurlansky.

45   "*Canarias* . . . steaming at top speed toward the captured fishing boat": https://

elpais.com/diario/2009/11/15/
espana/1258239601_850215.html.

45   **"2:20 a.m. on October 4,
Judge Baltasar Garzón":** https://
elpais.com/diario/2009/11/15/
espana/1258239601_850215.html.

46   Account of ransom delivery
and attempted recovery based on
interview with General Rodríguez.

47   **"Zapatero congratulated
all those who had worked to free
the *Alakrana*":** https://elpais.com/
elpais/2009/11/17/actualidad/
1258449418_850215.html.

47   **Judge's verdict, *Alakrana*
case:** http://estaticos.elmundo.es/
documentos/2011/05/03/sentencia_
alakrana.pdf

47   **Kidnapping of Albert Vilalta
Cambra, Alicia Gámez Guerrero,
and Roque Pascual Salazar in
Mauritania:** https://www.
theguardian.com/world/2009/nov/
30/spanish-aid-workers-kidnapped-
mauritania/.

47   **Details of Acció Solidaria
kidnapping:** http://www.elmundo
.es/elmundo/2009/12/08/barcelona/
1260272508.html.

48   Description of efforts to track
the movement of the hostages from
Mauritania through Mali via a senior
CNI official who asked not be
identified.

49   **Mustafa Chafi:** http://www
.catalannews.com/society-science/
item/the-2-catalans-kidnapped-by-
al-qaeda-are-back-to-barcelona;

http://www.jeuneafrique.com/mag/
491459/politique/sahel-quels-sont-
les-liens-entre-les-jihadistes-et-
moustapha-chafi-ex-conseiller-de-
compaore/.

49   **Release of Alicia Gámez:**
https://elpais.com/elpais/2010/03/
10/actualidad1268212618_850215
.html; https://elpais.com/diario/
2010/03/12/espana/1268348402_
850215.html.

50   **"millions of dollars in
ransom was paid":** https://elpais
.com/elpais/2010/08/22/actualidad/
1282465020_850215.html.

50   **"may have been fronted by
the government of Burkina Faso":**
http://www.dw.com/en/al-qaeda-
releases-spanish-hostages/a-
5936175.

52   **"voters returned the
conservatives to power":** https://
www.washingtonpost.com/world/
europe/spains-conservative-
declare-victory-in-election/2011/
11/20/gIQADBpZfN_story.html.

52   **Spanish hostages that
have come home alive:** https://
na-production.s3.amazonaws.com/
documents/hostage-paper-final.pdf.

53   **"Held Hostage:** Analyses
of Kidnapping Across Time and
Among Jihadist Organizations."
https://ctc.usma.edu/wp-content/
uploads/2015/12/Held-Hostage
reportc2.pdf.

54   **"To Pay Ransom Or Not To
Pay Ransom? An Examination of
Western Hostage Policies."** 2017
New America Foundation study

178 https://na-production.s3.amazonaws
.com/documents/hostage-paper-
final.pdf.

**55   Graeme Wood, "Ransoms:
The Real Cost."** http://www
.nybooks.com/daily/2014/11/19/
ransoms-real-cost/

55   Edwin Dyer: https://www
.theguardian.com/uk/2009/jun/03/
edwin-dyer-hostage-killed-al-qaida

**56   "Taliban claimed they used
the $10 million ransom":** http://
www.telegraph.co.uk/news/world
news/1566163/Taliban-use-hostage-
cash-to-fund-UK-blitz.html.

**56   "Karzai then went on
television to declare he would never
negotiate again":** *The Fixer*, http://
www.thefixerdocumentary.com/.

**56   "kill the hostage with 'the
lowest rank':** https://abcnews.go
.com/International/osama-bin-
laden-letters-show-paranoid-
micromanager-hiding/
story?id=37297647.

57   "A *New York Times* **analysis
put the number at $125 million over
the same period":** https://www
.nytimes.com/2014/07/30/world/
africa/ransoming-citizens-europe-
becomes-al-qaedas-patron.html.

**57   "The group . . . expanded its
smuggling operations using
existing routes":** https://www
.newyorker.com/magazine/2015/12/
14/trafficking-in-terror.

59   MRTA: https://dialogo-
americas.com/en/articles/peruvian-
armed-forces-ready-amazonlog.

59   Sendero Luminoso: http://
www.dw.com/es/despu%C3%A9s-
de-25-a%C3%B1os-qu%C3%A9-
queda-de-sendero-luminoso/a-
40476915.

CHAPTER THREE

**62   I interviewed Doug Milne in
London on July 28, 2017, and then
again on October 24.** Additional
background on the relationship
between the British government and
the London-based security industry
is drawn from contemporaneous news
accounts, cited below, and *Ransom*
by Ann Hagedorn Auerbach. For
Thatcher and K & R, see pp. 215–217.
For the police official quoted in the
Guiness case see p. 216.

**64   "Julian Radcliffe, an
insurance broker with Hogg
Robinson":** https://www.
theguardian.com/business/1999/
mar/02/14.

**64   "In 1982, Control Risks
became an independent company":**
https://www.theguardian.com/
business/2010/mar/14/kroll-
control-risks-bidding-war.

**65   "By the early 1980s,
hostage-taking was exploding
in Latin America":** https://link.
springer.com/chapter/10.1007/
978-1-349-18754-6_14.

65   *pesca milagrosa:* http://www
.nytimes.com/1999/06/03/world/
fishing-for-ransom-colombian-
rebels-cast-net-wide.html.

66   Special Contingency Risks:
https://blog.willis.com/2012/07/

piracy-in-south-east-asia/; https://
www.economist.com/blogs
schumpeter/2013/06/kidnap-and-
ransom-insurance.

67   **Hiscox/Control Risks:**
https://www.hiscoxspecialrisks
.com/control-risks

67   **AIG/NYA:** http://www.aig
.com/content/dam/aig/america-
canada/us/documents/business/
management-liability/nya-crisis-
prevention-and-response-brochure
.pdf.

67   **K & R Market:** https://www
.theguardian.com/world/2014/aug
/25/murky-world-hostage-
negotiations-price-ever-right-
insurance; https://www.cognizant
.com/whitepapers/Kidnap-and-
Ransom-Insurance-At-an-
Inflection-Point-codex1575.pdf.

68   Doug Milne's clients' killing
in Colombia based on personal
account.

69   **Margaret Thatcher's no**
concessions policy: http://news.bbc
.co.uk/2/hi/uk_news/3702574.stm.

69   **Jennifer Guinness**
kidnapping: http://articles.latimes
.com/1986-04-10/news/mn-3446_1_
jennifer-guinness; https://books
.google.com/books?id=S2SNAw
AAQBAJ&pg=PT27&lpg=PT27&dq=
guinness+jennifer+control+risks&
source=bl&ots=IozKnWMjio&sig=
kSDUkJ8dJ4NWnvIeIznu
B2vl8SM&hl=en&sa=X&ved=0ah
UKEwjB56u5vcTYAhVQkeAKHZo
ZAf4Q6AEIJzAA#v=onepage&q=
guinness%20jennifer%20control%

20risks&f=false; See also Ransom,
cited above.

69   The study cited by Milne was
published in *The Post*, an insurance
industry trade magazine, in May
1986. It argued that "the existence of
an insurance policy ensures that the
authorities are informed as soon as
the kidnap takes place. . . . Kidnap
insurance is thus more likely to result
in less money getting into the hands
of terrorists organizations."

70   **"Italy, for example, passed**
a law in 1991": http://www.nytimes
.com/1998/02/01/world/italian-ban-
on-paying-kidnappers-stirs-anger
.html.

70   **"like the more than $20**
million ransom allegedly paid to
win the freedom of Mexican banker
Alfredo Harp Helú in 1994": http://
www.nytimes.com/1994/06/25/
world/family-of-kidnapped-
mexican-financier-agrees-to-
ransom.html.

71   **Proscribed terrorist groups**
in the U.S. and UK: https://www
.state.gov/j/ct/rls/other/des/
123085.htm, https://www.gov.uk/
government/publications/
proscribed-terror-groups-or-
organisations—2.

72   **Masefield AG vs. Amlin**
Corporate Member: http://law
.unimelb.edu.au/__data/assets/pdf_
file/0007/1703482/35_2_14.pdf.

73   **David Rohde kidnapping:**
http://www.nytimes.com/2009/
10/18/world/asia/18hostage.html?
pagewanted=all; https://www

180   .nytimes.com/interactive/projects/
held-by-the-taliban/#part-5; See
also *A Rope and a Prayer.*

**75   Amanda Lindhout
kidnapping:** https://www
.theguardian.com/world/2009/
nov/26/kidnapped-journalists-
freed-somalia; See also *A House
in the Sky.*

75   Through my work at CPJ,
I was involved behind the scenes in
the Lindhout case, and some of my
observations are drawn from that
experience. Additional detail is
from a *Planet Ransom* interview,
https://www.npr.org/templates/
transcript/transcript.php?storyId=
548026545; See also: http://
nationalpost.com/news/canada/
i-owe-my-life-to-the-people-
who-paid-my-ransom-but-should-
our-government-pay-ransoms-no-
i-dont-think-so/wcm/eb6f2bfb-
bc94-498a-993e-ab3f77b28575.

75   While Canada and Australia
are firmly in the no concessions
camp, both appear to take a more
flexible approach than either the
U.S. and U.K. Australia will facilitate
private ransom payments of up to
$250,000, according to the New
America study. Canada has offered
economic assistance in exchange
for the release of its nationals and is
reported to have facilitated a ransom
of the over $1 million for the release
of the two Canadian diplomats
taken captive by Al Qaeda in Niger
in 2008 (see Chapter Two, page
56). Following the beheading of a
Canadian hostage in the Philippines
in 2016, Prime Minister Justin
Trudeau declared "Canada does

not and will not pay ransom to
terrorists, directly or indirectly"
because doing so "would endanger
the lives of every single one of the
millions of Canadians who live,
work, and travel around the globe
every single year." But a former
senior official, Gar Pardy, was
dismissive. "It's just something
governments say," Pardy declared.
"You always pay. It's as simple as
that." See Terry Glavin, "Canada
Does Not Pay Ransom . . . Except
When We Do," *National Post,* April
27, 2016. http://nationalpost.com/
opinion/terry-glavin-canada-does-
not-pay-ransom-to-terrorists-
except-when-we-do.

**76   "Cameras caught him
telling Defense Secretary Leon
Panetta 'good job tonight'":**
https://www.cbsnews.com/news/
obamas-good-job-a-public-wink-
on-seal-secret/

**76   "The kidnappers had
initially demanded $10 million,
and had recently rejected a $1
million offer":** https://www
.washingtonpost.com/world/
national-security/us-forces-
rescue-kidnapped-aid-workers-
jessica-buchanan-and-poul-
hagen-thisted-in-somalia/2012/
01/25/gIQA7WopPQ_story.html?
utm_term=.3415d5bad9ef

**77   Michael Scott Moore
kidnapping:** https://www.
theguardian.com/world
/2015/jun/02/my-977-days-held-
hostage-by-somali-pirates;
additional detail from a personal
interview with a source close to
the Moore case.

77   **Steve Farrell raid:** http://
www.nytimes.com/2009/09/09/
world/asia/09rescue.html

78   Detail about a ransom having
been negotiated prior to the rescue
attempt via a confidential source.

78   I interviewed Ollie Tebbutt on
November 9, 2017. Additional details
are drawn from Jude Tebbutt's *A Long
Walk Home.*

81   All of the dozen or so security
consultants I interviewed—in the
U.S., UK, Canada, and a number
of European countries—asked to
speak on background, meaning
I cannot quote them by name. I
agreed because of the sensitivity
of their work and because I wanted
them to speak frankly. This section
represents a consensus of their
views.

CHAPTER FOUR

85   I interviewed David Cohen on
December 18, 2017 and January 12,
2018. I interviewed Brian Jenkins on
September 27. I had various meetings
and phone interviews with Gary
Noesner over the course of 2017.
The account of the formulation of
NSPD-12 is based on interviews with
several sources with direct
knowledge who asked not to be
identified.

85   **"administration officials
called David S. Cohen their
'financial Batman'":** https://www
.nytimes.com/2014/10/22/business/
international/enforcer-at-treasury-
is-first-line-of-attack-against-isis
.html?_r=0.

85   **FARC, Al Qaeda, and Islamic
State funders:** https://www
.theatlantic.com/news/archive/2016/
07/farc-cocaine-colombia/489551/,
https://www.washingtonpost.com/
world/national-security/islamic-
charity-officials-gave-millions-to-
al-qaeda-us-says/2013/12/22
e0c53ad6-69b8-11e3-a0b9-
249bbb34602c_story.html?utm_
term=.58e80984dee2, https://www
.huffingtonpost.com/daniel-wagner/
why-there-is-no-stopping-_b_
7518012.html.

86   **David Cohen's speech at
Chatham House:** https://www
.treasury.gov/press-center/press-
releases/Pages/tg1726.aspx.

87   **Black September's 1973
kidnapping in Sudan:** David Carlton
and Carlo Schaerf, *International
Terrorism and World Security*
https://books.google.com/
books?id=vXJKCAAAQBAJ&pg=
PA42&lpg=PA42&dq=march+1973+
black+september+pakistan+saudi+
embassy&source=bl&ots=_da_
kOsAEF&sig=wUp8J7UW_
GqfoEcD1TFjqBXvrng&hl=
en&sa=X&ved=0ahUKEwiAyt-
FwsbYAhVJUd8KHb9LAPkQ6A
EIMzAC#v=onepage&q=march%
201973%20black%20september%
20pakistan%20saudi%20embassy
&f=false; https://news.google.com/
newspapers?id=Mt0qAAAAIBA
J&sjid=HXwFAAAAIBAJ&pg=
1650,637152.

87   **President Nixon's press
conference:** http://www.presidency
.ucsb.edu/ws/index.php?pid=4123.

182   90   It's worth noting that American policymakers have been engaged to a certain extent with the concessions/no concessions debate since the birth of the Republic. When American sailors were captured by Algerian pirates in 1785, Thomas Jefferson spoke out against paying ransom because he believed it would encourage further kidnappings. Yet in 1791, Congress authorized $40,000 in ransom. The pirates rejected the offer and continued to seize American vessels. Finally, after years of arduous negotiation, the U.S. Congress agreed to pay $585,000 for the release of American sailors. Some were held in deplorable conditions for over a decade.

90   For history of the U.S. no concessions policy see "Does the U.S. No-Concessions Policy Deter Kidnappings of Americans," by Brian Michael Jenkins. https://www.rand .org/pubs/perspectives/PE277.html.

91   TWA Flight 847 account and Iran Contra description from Buhite, *Lives at Risk*, p. 195.

91   **Geneva Conventions' rule on prisoner exchanges:** https://ihl-databases.icrc.org/applic/ihl/ihl.nsf/ 7c4d08d9b287a4214125673900 3e63bb/6fef854a3517b75ac125641 e004a9e68.

91   **Federal Kidnap Act:** https:// news.google.com/newspapers?id= sIo1AAAAIBAJ&sjid=w6sFAAA AIBAJ&pg=2635%2C754661.

91   *New York Times* **Gary Noesner profile:** http://www

.nytimes.com/2002/02/19/us/ nation-challenged-hostages-fbi-veteran-hostage-negotiations-helped-reshaping-us.html.

91   **"President Reagan declared, 'America will never make concessions to terrorists'":** http://www.presidency.ucsb.edu/ ws/inde.php?pid=38789.

92   **NSPD-12:** https://fas.org/ irp/offdocs/nspd/index.html; http:// www.nytimes.com/2002/02/19/ us/nation-challenged-hostages-fbi-veteran-hostage-negotiations-helped-reshaping-us.html.

94   **"Abu Sayyaf kept the $300,000 but the hostages were not released":** http://abcnews .go.com/International/story?id= 79955&page=1

94   **"In 2007, fourteen Abu Sayyaf members were convicted in a Philippine court":** http://www .washingtonpost.com/wp-dyn/ content/article/2007/12/05/ AR2007120502923_pf.html.

96   John Otis, *Law of the Jungle*; See also *Hostage Nation: Colombia's Guerrilla Army and the Failed War on Drugs* by Jorge Enrique Botero, Karin Hayes, and Victoria Bruce.

96   **Kidnapping of Ingrid Betancourt:** https://www .theguardian.com/world/2010/sep/ 18/ingrid-betancourt-i-still-have-nightmares.

96   Vice President Francisco (Pacho) Santos was kidnapped by Pablo Escobar and the Medellín

Cartel, and his experience was chronicled in Gabriel García Márquez's *News of Kidnapping*. Santos went on to help found a civil society organization, La Fundación País Libre, to advocate for the rights of hostages and lead public mobilizations to denounce the crime. The organization was disbanded in 2017 as the peace process with FARC and the overall reduction in the crime rate led to a dramatic reduction in kidnapping. The father of Colombian president Álvaro Uribe was killed by FARC in a botched kidnapping attempt carried out in 1983.

97   **February 2003 kidnapping of American contractors by FARC:** http://content.time.com/time/world/article/0,8599,1735671,00.html.

97   **"the French government tried to negotiate a ransom for Betancourt":** https://www.lexpress.fr/actualite/monde/ingrid-betancourt-la-france-aurait-paye-une-rancon-en-2003_525532.html.

98   **"France dispatched a hospital plane":** https://www.lexpress.fr/actualite/monde/le-calvaire-d-ingrid-betancourt_471888.html.

98   **Betancourt's release:** http://www.lepoint.fr/actualites-monde/2008-07-02/reactions-florence-aubenas-c-est-noel-en-juillet/924/0/257472.

99   **Botched raid for Michel Germaneau:** http://content.time.com/time/world/article/0,8599,2006463,00.html.

99   **Execution of Michel**   183
Germaneau: http://content.time.com/time/world/article/0,8599,2006463,00.html; Stephen Harmon, *Terror and Insurgency in the Sahara-Sahel Region* https://books.google.com/books?id=htm1CwAAQBAJ&pg=PA162&lpg=PA162&dq=abu+zeid+execution+michel+germaneau&source=bl&ots=pWu098xnOV&sig=4ftVBhYTR_ZAhl6TOMW-FOYo-hM&hl=en&sa=X&ved=0ahUKEwja9KKn2LTYAhXSSN8KHVCSA-8Q6AEINzAE#v=onepage&q=abu%20zeid%20execution%20michel%20germaneau&f=false.

99   **Kidnapping of Hervé Ghesquière and Stéphane Taponier:** http://www.liberation.fr/planete/2011/06/29/herve-ghesquiere-et-stephane-taponier-sont-libres_746058; http://www.lemonde.fr/international/article/2012/09/21/le-livre-de-l-ancien-otage-herve-ghesquiere-ravive-la-polemique-avec-l-armee_1763671_3210.html; http://france3-regions.francetvinfo.fr/hauts-de-france/2014/12/08/herve-ghesquiere-ancien-otage-candamne-en-appel-pour-diffamation-609068.html; http://www.lemonde.fr/societe/article/2011/06/30/la-joie-d-herve-ghesquiere-et-stephane-taponier_1542832_3224.html.

100   **Aubenas's appeal:** http://www.lemonde.fr/idees/article/2010/06/29/herve-ghesquiere-et-stephane-taponier-nous-devons-parler-d-eux-chaque-jour_1380291_3232.html.

184   100   **RSF Action:** https://rsf.org/fr/actualites/liberation-dherve-ghesquiere-et-stephane-taponier-apres-un-et-demi-de-captivite.

101   **Tour de France:** http://www.programme-tv.net/news/tv/10072-200-jours-de-captivite-pour-les-journalistes-otages-en-afghanistan/.

101   **"Detailed account in** *The Daily Beast*": http://www.thedailybeast.com/articles/2011/07/01/taliban-s-french-hostages-how-they-were-freed.html.

102   **UN Security Council Resolution 1904:** http://www.un.org/press/en/2009/sc9825.doc.htm.

103   **"Cameron secured a pledge from all its members not to pay ransom":** https://www.ft.com/content/10cc2546-d832-11e2-b4a4-00144feab7de.

103   **"In January 2014, when the UK followed up on the consensus it had built at the G-8 Summit":** https://www.un.org/press/en/2014/sc11262.doc.htm.

CHAPTER FIVE

104   The account of Motka's kidnapping is based on several interviews with Federico Motka, both in person and by phone, which took place in July 2017. I did a follow-up interview in October 2017. I spoke to Mike Haines via skype in October 17. The description of the rise of ISIS is from *Black Flag* by Joby Warrick and numerous journalistic accounts cited below.

105   **"Haines, a forty-four-year-old former British soldier":** http://www.telegraph.co.uk/news/obituaries/11095290/David-Haines-obituary.html.

106   **Atmeh refugee camp:** https://www.theguardian.com/world/2014/feb/18/syrian-refugee-camp-township-atmeh.

106   **"several masked fighters with Kalashnikovs":** http://www.independent.co.uk/news/world/middle-east/david-haines-exclusive-witness-describes-the-moment-isis-militants-seized-british-aid-worker-9712916.html.

108   **"two Italian aid workers kidnapped in Baghdad were ransomed":** http://www.washingtonpost.com/wp-dyn/articles/A55850-2004Sep28.html?referrer=email.

109   **"The following year, a well-known Italian journalist, Giuliana Sgrena, was also freed":** http://www.cnn.com/2005/WORLD/europe/03/06/italy.iraq/index.html.

109   **2013 release of an Italian and a Belgian:** https://www.reuters.com/article/us-italy-syria-journalist/italian-and-belgian-freed-after-being-kidnapped-in-syria-idUSBRE9870EG20130908.

111   **Kidnapping of Didier François and Eduard Elias:** https://www.ladepeche.fr/article/2014/04/21/1867363-ex-otages-didier-francois-raconte-des-simulacres-d-executions.html.

111 **"described his eloquent reports as 'written radio'"**: https://laregledujeu.org/2013/07/16/13799/pour-didier-francois/.

111 **Eduard Elias:** http://www.reportagebygettyimages.com/edouard-elias/.

112 **Mehdi Nenmouche:** http://www.france24.com/en/20161103-belgium-extradition-france-brussels-jewish-museum-shooting-nemmouche.

113 I interviewed Javier Espinosa and Mónica Prieto in northern Spain on July 15, 2017. I relied also on their book, *Siria: El pais de las almas rotas*, along with *The ISIS Hostage* by Puk Damsgård.

114 The jailer that the hostages called "George" was later identified as Mohamed Emwazi. He was killed in a U.S. drone strike in 2015. Confusingly he was dubbed "Jihadi John" in the media. Another member of the "Beatles," Aine Davis, a British national, was arrested in Turkey and is currently serving a seven-year sentence. http://www.telegraph.co.uk/news/2017/05/09/british-isil-jihadist-member-beatles-terror-cell-convicted-turkey/.

114 On February 16, 2018 the families of the American hostages murdered by ISIS published an op-ed in *The New York Times* entitled "Justice for Our Children, Killed by ISIS." The article was written in response to the capture of Alexanda Kotey and El Shafee Elsheikh. Two members of the "Beatles" who had

been detained by Kurdish forces in Northern Syria. The families called for the men to be brought to the U.S. to face trial. https://www.nytimes.com/2018/02/16/opinion/justice-isis-trial.html.

115 While in custody, ElSheikh was interviewed by journalist Jenan Moussa, who asked him to respond to the accusations of his involvement in kidnapping, torture, and murder of hostages. ElSheikh expressed no remorse, defended slavery, and said he would only answer specific questions in the context of a legal trial. https://www.memri.org/tv/british-isis-beatle-dont-denounce-slavery-nothing-beats-west-for-corruption/transcript.

116 I interviewed Pedro J. Ramírez in Madrid in July 2017.

116 **"Espinosa had survived the shelling of the press center in Homs"**: http://www.reportagebygettyimages.com/edouard-elias/.

116 **Assassination of José Luis López de Lacalle:** https://cpj.org/data/people/jose-luis-lopez-de-la-calle/.

116 **Death of Julio Anguita:** http://www.cnn.com/2003/WORLD/europe/04/07/sprj.irq.journalists.killed/

116 **Death of Julio Fuentes:** https://cpj.org/data/people/julio-fuentes/

116 **"he left in 1989 to found a new daily, *El Mundo*"**: https://

186 www.theguardian.com/world/2014/feb/09/el-mundo-pedro-j-ramirez-departure-spain.

116 **"In 1989, officials in Spain's Socialist government leaked a sex tape":** https://www.nytimes.com/2014/02/03/business/media/ousted-el-mundo-editor-assails-government.html.

116 **Agatha Ruiz de la Prada:** https://www.vanitatis.elconfidencial.com/tags/temas/divorcio-agatha-ruiz-de-la-prada-y-pedro-j-ramirez-19079/.

118 **Prieto's press conference in Beirut:** https://www.theguardian.com/world/2013/dec/10/spanish-journalist-javier-espinosa-kidnap-syria.

118 **"Pedro J. Ramírez was forced out as editor of *El Mundo*":** https://www.nytimes.com/2014/02/03/business/media/ousted-el-mundo-editor-assails-government.html.

120 **Assassination of Sergei Gorbunov:** https://www.nytimes.com/2014/10/26/world/middleeast/horror-before-the-beheadings-what-isis-hostages-endured-in-syria.html?_r=1

121 **Release of Espinosa and García Vilanova:** https://www.theguardian.com/world/2014/mar/30/spanish-journalists-javier-espinosa-ricardo-villanova-garcia-freed-syria.

121 **"the hostages were lucky to be French":** https://www.irishtimes.com/news/world/we-re-lucky-to-be-french-say-journalists-freed-in-syria-1.1768352.

122 **"Handled by MSF directly":** https://www.nytimes.com/interactive/2014/10/24/world/middleeast/the-fate-of-23-hostages-in-syria.html.

122 **"the Italian government paid an estimated $11 million":** https://www.theguardian.com/world/2015/jan/15/two-italian-aid-workers-freed-syria.

122 *Al Jazeera*'s "Hostage Business" details ransom paid for Italian aid workers http://www.aljazeera.com/investigations/hostagebusiness.html.

123 **Failed raid to save Foley and Sotloff:** https://www.newyorker.com/news/news-desk/inside-failed-raid-free-foley-sotloff; additional information from several sources knowledgeable about the events.

124 **Foley execution:** video https://leaksource.wordpress.com/2014/08/19/graphic-video-islamic-state-beheads-american-journalist-james-foley/.

125 **ISIS demands for Kayla Mueller:** http://abcnews.go.com/International/timeline-kayla-mueller-isis-captivity/story?id=41398733.

126 **Death of Kayla Mueller:** https://www.nytimes.com/2015/02/07/world/middleeast/isis-claims-american-hostage-killed-by-jordanian-retaliation-bombings.html.

126   **May 2015 raid to kill Abu Sayyaf:** http://www.cnn.com/2015/05/16/middleeast/syria-isis-us-raid/index.html.

126   **Testimony from Umm Sayyaf:** http://abcnews.go.com/International/wife-isis-figure-charged-american-woman-kayla-muellers/story?id=36796458.

126   **Mark Mitchell's comments to hostages' families in May 2014:** http://docs.house.gov/meetings/FA/FA18/20151117/104202/HHRG-114-FA18-Wstate-FoleyD-20151117.pdf.

128   **"Bradley and former FBI agent Ali Soufan traveled to Qatar":** https://www.newyorker.com/magazine/2015/07/06/five-hostages

128   **Theo Padnos's release:** https://www.nytimes.com/2014/08/25/world/middleeast/peter-theo-curtis-held-by-qaeda-affiliate-in-syria-is-freed-after-2-years.html.

129   In the May 2018 interview with Al Arabiya. Padnos said his kidnappers told him they were hoping to get a $20 million ransom and spoke openly about their relationship with Qatar. Following his release, Padnos met with senior Qatari officials in Doha, and told them that by financing Al-Nusra Front they were destroying Syria. Qatar's Foreign Minister was unperturbed, according to Padnos, telling him. "we know them very well and we have confidence in them." See http://english.alarabiya.net/en/webtv/programs/death-making/2018/05/14/

Ex-Nusra-Front-hostage-Theo-Padnos-Qatar-ransom-payouts-tactic-to-fund-terror.html.

130   **2015 LSE Lecture:** http://www.lse.ac.uk/Events/2015/03/20150305t1830vOT/Why-We-Should-Talk-to-Terrorists.

CHAPTER SIX

132   The description of the meeting with President Obama comes from Diane and John Foley. I interviewed them on several occasions, including during a visit to their home in Rochester, New Hampshire on March 31, 2017.

133   **Foley family goes public:** https://cpj.org/2013/01/family-of-seized-us-reporter-seeks-his-release-in.php.

134   **Lecture from Mark Mitchell, May 2014:** http://docs.house.gov/meetings/FA/FA18/20151117/104202/HHRG-114-FA18-Wstate-FoleyD-20151117.pdf; I reached out to Mitchell, who during 2017 served as Acting Assistant Secretary of Defense, but he did not respond to requests to be interviewed. He told *Al Jazeera* in a 2015 interview that he did not threaten the families, but wanted to make them aware of the legal risk of paying ransom. "It's a always a priority to recover American citizens," Mitchell said. "But it's not always the highest priority." http://www.aljazeera.com/investigations/hostagebusiness.html

134   Obama's response to the Foley murder is described by Ben Rhodes

188   in his memoir, *The World As it Is* (New York: Random House, 2017), pp. 294–296.

136   **"I want to continue Jim's work":** https://www.youtube.com/watch?v=2IwdVKXgGJg

136   **Doug Frantz at the Newseum:** http://www.newseum.org/event/the-news-we-could-lose-new-threats-to-journalism-and-press-freedom/

137   The account of the Hostage Policy Review is based on interviews with four participants, including Lisa Monaco, who I met on May 17, 2017 at her office at NYU Law School. See also Jere Van Dyk, *The Trade*.

137   **2014 U.S. hostage policy review:** https://obamawhitehouse.archives.gov/the-press-office/2015/06/24/fact-sheet-us-government-hostage-policy

138   **"Fusion cell":** https://www.fbi.gov/news/stories/hostage-recovery-fusion-cell-established.

138   **Kidnapping is a federal crime:** https://www.justice.gov/usam/criminal-resource-manual-1034-kidnapping-federal-jurisdiction.

140   **Special Envoy for Hostage Affairs:** https://www.nytimes.com/2016/09/12/us/politics/in-policy-shift-us-includes-families-in-hostage-rescue-efforts.html.

141   **"our top priority is the safe and rapid recovery of American hostages":** https://obamawhitehouse.archives.gov/the-press-office/2015/06/24/statement-president-us-governments-hostage-policy-review.

142   **Bowe Bergdahl exchange:** https://www.nytimes.com/2014/06/01/us/bowe-bergdahl-american-soldier-is-freed-by-taliban.html?_r=0.

142   **"National Security Advisor Susan Rice claimed Bergdahl had served with 'honor and distinction'":** https://www.youtube.com/watch?v=rp3fDThUlRY.

142   **Bergdahl family in Rose Garden:** https://www.washingtonpost.com/blogs/post-partisan/wp/2014/06/04/after-bergdahls-release-a-sickening-spectacle-in-the-rose-garden/?utm_term=.2a885bcd31b7.

143   **"Then there was the Jason Rezaian case in Iran":** https://www.washingtonpost.com/world/middle_east/post-reporter-rezaian-flies-to-us-after-release-by-iran-checkups-in-germany/2016/01/22/b47273ba-c09e-11e5-bcda-62a36b394160_story.html.

144   **Mike McGarrity named fusion cell director:** https://www.fbi.gov/news/stories/hostage-recovery-fusion-cell-established

145   **Terry Anderson:** http://www.cnn.com/2016/02/09/world/terry-anderson-hostage-rewind/index.html.

145   I interviewed Jim O'Brien in Washington, D.C. on March 16, 2017.

145   **"Jim O'Brien was appointed as the first Special Presidential Envoy for Hostage Affairs":** https://diplopundit.net/2015/09/01/president-obama-appoints-james-obrien-as-first-special-presidential-envoy-for-hostage-affairs/.

145   **Release of David Rohde:** https://www.csmonitor.com/1995/1121/21015.html

147   **Hostage UK:** https://hostageus.org/about/our-people/.

148   **New America Foundation, "To Pay Ransom Or Not To Pay Ransom":** https://www.newamerica.org/international-security/policy-papers/pay-ransom-or-not/.

153   "Kidnapped: The Ethics of Ransom Payment," by Jeffrey W. Howard in the *Journal of Applied Philosophy,* May, 2017 https://onlinelibrary.wiley.com/doi/abs/10.1111/japp.12272. See also "Does the U.S. No Concessions Policy Deter Kidnappings of Americans," by Brian Michael Jenkins, RAND, 2017 https://www.rand.org/pubs/perspectives/PE277.html.

158   **"Qatar paid hundreds of millions of dollars":** https://www.usnews.com/news/world/articles/2017-04-27/qatar-denies-trying-to-pay-ransom-money-to-free-hostages-in-iraq

161   Former FBI agent, author and security analyst Ali Soufan suggested the National Security framework.

162   For a more detailed discussion of media blackouts see my 2015 book, *The New Censorship.*

Columbia Global Reports is a publishing imprint from Columbia University that commissions authors to do original on-site reporting around the globe on a wide range of issues. The resulting novella-length books offer new ways to look at and understand the world that can be read in a few hours. Most readers are curious and busy. Our books are for them.

Subscribe to Columbia Global Reports and get six books a year in the mail in advance of publication. globalreports.columbia.edu/subscribe

Pipe Dreams: The Plundering of Iraq's Oil Wealth
Erin Banco

Never Remember: Searching for Stalin's Gulags in Putin's Russia
Masha Gessen and Misha Friedman

High-Speed Empire: Chinese Expansion and the Future of Southeast Asia
Will Doig

Saudi America: The Truth About Fracking and How It's Changing the World
Bethany McLean

The Nationalist Revival: Trade, Immigration, and the Revolt Against Globalization
John B. Judis

The Curse of Bigness: Antitrust in the New Gilded Age
Tim Wu

31192021615024